SUDDENL

SUDDENLY SINGLE

A guide for men and women coping with
bereavement, separation or divorce

Mary Wilson

COLUMBUS BOOKS
LONDON

Acknowledgements

I would like to acknowledge all those who believed in this book and encouraged, helped and cajoled me into finishing it, and particularly all the people who filled in my questionnaire with such courage and honesty. Some of them are quoted, though not under their real names. I lost count of the number of people who filled in the questionnaire. It was rather like a chain letter: people would photostat it and pass it on to all their friends.

I would like to thank all the organizations and professional people who kindly gave me their time and concern, and also ACT Ltd for the Apricot xi computer, Amanda Barrington-Smyth, Daphne Broadhead, Pauline Chandler, John Clark, Russell Conway, Dr Anne Cobbe, Dr David Delvin, Nigel Edwards, Tony Eldridge, Stella Groschel, Pauline Hutchinson, Benita Kyle, Brian Loftus, The Reverend David Meara, Darrell Nightingirl, Robert Pargitter, Shelley Power, Joscelyn Richards, Tony Satchell, Arthur Smith, Barbara Stuart-Smith and Renne Walker.

M.W.

Copyright © 1985 Mary Wilson

First published in Great Britain in 1985 by
Columbus Books
Devonshire House, 29 Elmfield Road, Bromley, Kent BR1 1LT

Typeset by Inforum Ltd, Portsmouth
Printed and bound by
Richard Clay plc, Bungay, Suffolk

British Library Cataloguing in Publication Data

Wilson, Mary
Suddenly single: a guide for men and women coping
   with bereavement, separation or divorce.
   1. Divorces—Life skills guides
   2. Widowers—Life skills guides   3. Widows
   —Life skills guides
   I. Title
   306.8'8   HQ814
   ISBN 0 86287 181 6

Contents

Introduction

Perhaps you are reading this book because you have been plunged into a single state, or you are pondering the consequences of becoming single by leaving your partner. You might be wondering what it will be like on your own, whether you will be able to cope and what problems you will have to face. This book will attempt to help you through this difficult, traumatic and often perplexing time.

I have tried to cover as many as possible of the complexities you will face in making a new life for yourself: accepting that you are single; understanding loneliness; coping with the family, colleagues and friends; looking after your health; understanding your children's feelings and helping them; changing your job or finding employment for the first time; moving house; finding professional help; giving a party; what to do about holidays. There are chapters on understanding your emotions, specific problems that may be faced by homosexuals, money, re-building your social life and so on.

At the back of the book are descriptions, names and addresses of the organizations and associations which can provide more specialized help, together with suggestions for other books, dealing with specific subjects in greater detail, which you may find helpful.

Incorporated in the text are case histories of people who have been through, and in most instances overcome, what you may be going through now. These experiences should help you realize that no problem is insurmountable. Although the situation comes to each individual as unique, and theirs alone, other people *have* felt the same and have had to cope with identical situations. I hope that reading their accounts will give you strength in the knowledge that you are not alone.

If you feel that there are problems with which you do not

want to bother your family, a friend, boss or colleagues, use *Suddenly Single* as your first advice centre: no book can take away the pain, or act as a cure for loneliness, but it might provide some practical tips and, even better, some inspiration, for you to grasp at in the first instance.

CHAPTER 1

A new beginning

Looking back through the history of man one can almost be made to believe that being single, after a certain age, is a heinous crime, a contagious disease or, at the very least, a sign of mental or physical defect.

This absurd view has probably done more damage to mankind than will ever be realized.

You are born 'you'. As a couple you are still 'you' and when, through chance or through choice, you find yourself alone again, you are still 'you'.

Many people find this difficult to achieve, at any stage of their life, and becoming suddenly single can devastate even the strongest. You are never really alone, but it can be extremely hard to realize that and re-discover yourself.

Our society is not, unfortunately, geared to single people. For all the so-called liberalism, permissiveness, and feminist movements of the past decade, legally, socially, and morally society is still attuned to the 'couple syndrome', and to the textbook family of two adults, of the opposite sex, with children.

Often your friends who are part of a couple can be unbelievably smug and unintentionally hurtful, forgetting that you feel different from them in many ways. Perhaps, if you think back, you might remember how you, for example, considered including a single person in some arrangement and then decided not to, because they were not part of a couple. When you yourself are single that realization is sharply brought home.

You cannot ignore these problems, but they are never insoluble. With understanding of what lies behind them they can eventually be eradicated.

TIME TO RE-ASSESS
This is a very positive stage in your life, although you may not realize it at the moment. Do not let it slip away.

Now you are on your own you have time to re-assess your life, the opportunity to alter it – if you want. You could change your job, or take up employment for the first time, try a new sport or hobby, go to places you have always dreamed of, move from the country to the city, or *vice versa*; or maybe just change your hairstyle and generally please yourself.

If you feel you want to make major changes it is wiser to wait some months before taking any drastic action. You may not be thinking clearly and rationally at first – although you may think you are – and you could make a big mistake if you act too quickly. When you feel happier within yourself, have recovered from the initial shock, have thought hard and long about where you want your life to go, then is the time to make those moves.

However depressed, despairing, hurt, angry, bewildered or just plain scared you may be feeling, it is vitally important to remember that these emotions will not last forever. Life will improve. You will eventually feel happier and through this experience become stronger, more fulfilled, and with a greater understanding of yourself.

But these changes in your life can occur only through your own efforts. Other people can help, give support, help to straighten out your emotions, but in the end you will have to pull yourself through alone.

The world does not stand still while you are suffering: only you can control the quality of your life.

USING PILLS AS A PROP

There is little point in becoming dependent on pills or drugs of any kind. For a short while you may need something to help you sleep, or to 'calm your nerves', but in the long run you will still have to cope with the problems that were getting you down in the first place. They will not miraculously disappear.

Nicola, 34, a mother with two children, went to her doctor after separating from her husband because she felt she needed something to calm her down.

'I couldn't sleep,' she recalled, 'and I was desperately worried because I had taken the kids away from him. My doctor . . . talked to me, gave me support, but when I asked for some pills to help me through, she told me that tablets solve nothing . . . I had to be tough. My children would survive the break-up, and so could I. After this long talk she did give me a packet of pills, but told me that she expected me to bring them back a week later unopened. I did exactly that. By talking to her, I realized I could cope and the children would be OK. All I had needed was my confidence boosted, not pills at all.'

OVERCOMING DESPAIR

It is very important to remember that you are not unique. There is always somebody in a worse position than you. This fact may not, initially, offer much comfort, but it can and does help. Many people have told me that reading about how others have coped has helped immensely.

It is easy to fall into the trap of self-indulgence, to wallow in your misery and predicament without trying to do anything to pull yourself out of it. Perhaps you can hear yourself saying, 'No one can feel as awful as I do, nobody understands, I can't bear to meet anyone, I can't go out, I can't get a job – nobody wants me.'

For a start there is no such word as 'can't'. Anything can be done with will-power and if tackled in the right way. For example, if you feel you cannot meet people, take it in small stages. Do not throw yourself straight into party-going. Undoubtedly in such an environment you would feel out of place, terrified, lonely and unloved. Instead, try inviting a friend or two round for a cup of coffee. Soon you will see that you can cope, and that other people do care for and love you.

If you have never worked before, there is nothing to stop you working now. Remember that 'work' need not only mean paid employment: all the voluntary organizations need as much help as they can get. If you look, you will eventually find something to suit your temperament. It is true that finding a job can be difficult, but that is no excuse for not trying. You might even find you enjoy the quest.

You might feel you will never be able to cope – with the children, finance, running the home – all on your own. Certainly it will demand a certain amount of organization and concentration, but it can be done, especially if you know where to ask for advice when you need it.

My own grandmother had five children when her husband died unexpectedly. She had never cooked – ever; never taken more of a decision than what to ask the cook to prepare for the day's meals, and was suddenly left on her own with three teenage daughters and a very young son. She learnt what to do because she had to, and she eventually found she enjoyed it. She learnt to decorate the house, became a marvellous cook and coped admirably. If you had asked her before her husband died if she would have been able to run home and children on her own, she would have replied, 'Never in a million years'. But she did.

A LITTLE HELP. . .

Many people are afraid to admit that they need help, need to talk to someone, or can benefit from others' advice. They feel it is a weakness in themselves that they need others. They may be embarrassed to talk to people about what is worrying them, not only to others but to themselves. They may even feel it is degrading to burden other people with their worries.

We all respond to, and need a little help from, our friends. Think of the times you may have been asked for advice, or have given up a few hours to listen to somebody else's worries. You were probably happy to do so, so why not ask the same of your friends if you need to?

COMING TO TERMS WITH YOUR FEELINGS

When you are left suddenly on your own, you are plunged into a new world, one where people react differently to you. You experience the gamut of feelings, some which may be quite unexpected. You are in a world on your own, after being two. You might have children with you – but that is not the same as having adult support, companionship and love.

You feel grief, loss, unhappiness, depression, hate, anger, regret, bitterness – or just nothing. You might feel any one of these emotions or all of them, possibly with an intensity you never imagined you were capable of feeling.

For you to come through this traumatic period of your life, to learn from it, grow from it, benefit from it – all experiences in life teach us something – you must understand the reasons for how you are feeling, work them out in your own mind and come to terms with them, accept them. Then you can leave them behind and go forward.

You will find out things about yourself you may have denied vehemently before. You will learn things about

4

yourself you dislike, or are proud of. All are part of the real you, and having discovered them, and therefore your inner self, you will have the strength to enter your new life ahead. It will be different from before, but it could turn out to be more fulfilling and more serene.

TALKING OUT THE EMOTION

Many people, especially those who are not used to looking deeply into themselves, find it hard to sort out their emotions after bereavement or divorce. If you cannot do this on your own, talk to someone who can help you put your feelings into perspective, and help you to find that inner you.

This someone else could be a friend, a relative or a parent – although parents are rarely the best people to ask because it is nearly impossible for them to be objective and not put forward their views and their personal desires. It could be one of the many conciliation or counselling services whose staff are trained to listen and advise, not judge or dictate. It could be a clergyman, a doctor or a psychologist.

Unfortunately, in our society, many people find it excessively difficult to talk frankly. To let your feelings out, to say what you really mean, can be a tremendous effort; and you may be even more reluctant to ask for help. Having to ask for help is sometimes seen as personal failure. For men, in particular, this attitude is instilled in them by their upbringing, and by social expectations that they will be strong and self-reliant.

For women it is intrinsically easier. They are brought up from birth to be able to ask for help all through their lives – from their parents, their teachers, their boyfriends, their husbands. Nobody thinks it odd or unusual if a woman needs to ask for help. Men, on the other hand, are expected to provide the shoulders to cry on, not to do the crying themselves.

Yet men have similar feelings, insecurities, and the same need – and right – to ask for help as much as any woman. You will hear people commenting on how well a woman is dealing with her problems, but you very rarely hear anyone comment on how well a man is bearing up to a similar problem.

Because of this social indoctrination men often find it unbearably hard, sometimes almost impossible, to admit that they need someone, to take the plunge to go to somebody for help. Even being able to talk honestly to a friend without feeling the need to brag that everything is rosy can take a tremendous amount of courage. That honest chat with a good friend could be just the help they need.

Dr Anne Cobbe, a general practitioner who has had experience of many distressed men and women coming to talk to her, has said: 'Everyone needs someone to talk to. They need help in sorting out the roundabouts of their thought processes. You can go round in circles without someone there to stop the confusion and point you in a logical direction. Men sometimes do cope better because they have been brought up to be the survivor and to be strong, but when they can't it is worse. Men can get depressed, quicker and deeper. They are not used to asking for help.'

It was shown, in a newspaper survey conducted two years ago (for the London *Daily Express*), that after a marriage break-up 62 per cent men suffered from depression and 12 per cent from minor illnesses.

And many people fail to appreciate that in cases where the wife is granted custody, the man is not only losing his partner but his children as well. He may have wanted to divorce his wife – but not his children, and that can have a devastating effect on a man. It can lead to feelings of guilt, as well as loss.

FEELINGS OF ABANDONMENT

When you suffer loss you can also feel abandoned and your feelings regress to old childhood fears, relating what has happened now to past bad experiences. It can be the same feeling as experienced on losing a parent. You feel alone and, like a child, you need someone to turn to, someone to look after you.

It can be very difficult to come to terms with these emotions, and often, instead of understanding or allowing yourself to feel them, you feel anger and guilt. It is important to give yourself permission to feel like this. Men, especially, experience difficulty coming to terms with regressive childhood feelings, as do basically stronger people who do not consider themselves as someone who needs to turn to others for help.

Joscelyn Richards, principal psychologist for the Nation-

Westall Local History Trails 1999

The Tynemouth Trail is on Sundays and Thursdays, 10.30 a.m.-12.30 p.m. Meet at Tynemouth Metro Station, outside the newsagents, on the following dates:-

Sundays
May 16 **June** 6, 13, 20, 27 **July** 4, 11, 18, 25 **August** 1, 8, 15, 22, 29 **September** 5

Thursdays
July 1, 8, 15, 22, 29 **August** 5, 12, 19, 26 **September** 2

The North Shields Trail is on Sundays and Tuesdays, 2 - 4 p.m. Meet at North Shields Library, Northumberland Square on the following dates:-

Sundays
May 16 **June** 6, 13, 20, 27 **July** 4, 11,18, 25 **August** 1, 8, 15, 22, 29 **September** 5

Tuesdays
July 6, 13, 20, 27 **August** 3, 10, 17, 24, 31

A special walk along the whole Westall Trail will take place on Wednesday 23 June, 6 - 9 p.m. Meet outside North Shields Library, Northumberland Square.

Visit the Westall website at www.norham.n-tyneside.sch.uk/westall/index.htm

Join a <u>FREE</u> guided tour around the

Westall Local History Trails

and learn about Tynemouth and North Shields

Robert Westall was the famous North Shields born author of "The Machine Gunners" and many other books, some about local places and events. The North Tyneside Library Service has produced a colourful leaflet about the author and the trail based on his life and his books. During 1999, there will be FREE guided tours around North Shields and Tynemouth to explore points of local interest and hear about Robert Westall.

You don't need to book - just turn up on the day!

All dates were correct at the time of publication, but please check nearer the time with North Shields Library on **0191 200 5424.**
Private Parties welcome - Groups can book a special trail

Tel: 0191 200 5424

al Health Service, sees the problem from a sociological standpoint: 'If the surrounding sub-culture is sympathetic it is made easier for the sufferer to express his grief. The weeping and wailing of some Latin or Eastern cultures may seem absurdly over the top, but being able to abandon themselves to grief, to get it out of their system, means their recovery time is a good deal shorter.

'The English, especially, tend to believe in the "stiff upper lip": you should not be distraught, you should not show your inner feelings, and because of this the time taken to sort out and work out your emotions can be prolonged. You must remember that grief has to get to the worst part before it will get better. People have their own internal rhythms of getting over something, but they must let them out, must experience them and not suppress those feelings.'

Another point she makes is that those who instigated the break-up rarely expect to experience feelings of loss. When these feelings emerge, often in the form of physical illnesses, or perhaps many months after the break, they come as quite a shock.

'People often feel anxious, cannot sleep, can't cope during the daytime or with their children, and they cannot find a reason for it. They may have separated from their spouse, which is what they wanted, or they have been through a very unhappy marriage and were relieved to be out of it. What they do not realize, very often, is that however much they disliked or were unhappy about their spouse, there must have been some feeling of love or attachment at one time, and because of this there will be a feeling of loss. It might not come out for some weeks or even months, and when it does it catches them unaware. They were dealing with the break-up perfectly well before. Why should they suddenly feel upset later on?

'But this little tiny bit of loss has to come out somewhere and be recognized, and these ignored feelings may come out as headaches, poor physical health, no resistance to colds. And this is when they need to talk to someone, to have an understanding and supportive person. Not someone who is going to say, don't be silly – you got over it OK, there is no reason for you to be feeling depressed, angry or bitter.'

You need to talk to someone who will give you support,

7

someone who will listen to you, feel with you, without telling you what to do; someone who will not be intrusive, but will bear with you as you work through your emotions.

You can talk to old friends who know you well, or new friends whom you might feel are more impartial. Friends can be a wonderful source of strength and comfort, or just listeners. Although they are not trained counsellors, they can help in many ways if they know you well, and because they can stand apart from the problems and see the wood from the trees, they can often find a line of action that you, being too emotionally involved, have completely missed.

Many people find it hard at first to cope with the practical side of life: shopping, writing letters, simple household tasks – it all becomes an enormous effort. A friend who can ease the pressure at this time can be of enormous emotional as well as practical support.

The first person you may turn to is your GP. You can either see him specifically to talk about your emotional problems, or arrange an appointment on the pretence of a small matter and then let your troubles out. Some people find this much easier than just starting in on what is worrying them most. Most doctors will be as helpful and sympathetic as they can, but one major drawback is their lack of time.

Psychologists can also be of help. If your doctor, or a counsellor, feels it is necessary for you to have someone more specialized in the workings of the mind they will refer you to one. Quite often, the knowledge that the psychologist does not know you – whereas your doctor does – can make it easier to explain how you are feeling.

You might think of turning to the church for help, though possibly not if you are going through a divorce. In the case of bereavement many people do turn to their local minister for strength and comfort, and will find spiritual help and human sympathy. Every clergyman will of course be glad to give help and understanding at any time, not only in times of grief.

However, people without religious convictions usually feel that they can hardly turn to their local priest or vicar in times of trouble. Perhaps they assume he will be judgemental and dictatorial, and unless they have had personal contact they will find it very difficult to ich him. Often they will only do so when they are desperate, when there is no one else to turn to.

Occasionally, it must be said, ministers of religion have taken such an opportunity to 'push' religion very strongly on the applicant, but such cases are rare. Most will be glad just to listen to your problems and try to help. And for a sympathetic and understanding ear, you could hardly do better.

If you feel guilty because you are breaking your marriage vows, but realize that the marriage is truly over, a priest can usually help you cope with your guilt and help you come to terms with it. There are now very few clergy who insist that marriage is forever, whatever the circumstances; but of course it depends on the individual, and if you have had contact with him before you will be able to judge whether he is the right person to be able to help you.

More suggestions for people and associations to turn to are given in Chapter 13.

ENJOYING YOUR OWN COMPANY

Now you are on your own, you have to learn new skills, to make decisions on your own, with nobody else there to help take the strain. It might seem hard, but it is not impossible.

From being lonely and feeling incapable in the face of so many decisions, unable, perhaps, even to decide what to have for breakfast, you will come to realize the joy of being independent. You can have those eggs poached instead of fried, as your partner always insisted on; you can get up early on a Sunday morning or lie in if you feel like it; you do not have to watch the snooker programme or the interviewer you hated; you can alter the times of your meals without a second thought.

You have the freedom to do exactly what you want, when you want and how you want.

Enjoy your new-found independence. Explore it and be grateful for it. Many people never get the chance.

The following two chapters deal with the specific problems that face a widow or widower (Chapter 2) and someone going through separation or divorce (Chapter 3). Although there is a popular view that both experience similar emotions, I have come to the conclusion that they are in fact very different. Of course people feel loss, and possibly also anger, resentment, bitterness or recrimination, in both situations, but these feelings are directed in different ways and need to be understood in their individual context.

CHAPTER 2

Bereavement

If you have just been widowed, coping with the immediate practicalities of death is a task for which you will probably want to enlist the help of a member of the family, a friend or a solicitor. Offers of help, you will find, come from all quarters at such a time; do not be afraid of taking people at their word.

ESSENTIAL PROCEDURES

Immediately after the death, if it occurs at home, the family doctor and a minister of religion, if the religion of the deceased so dictates (one who was known to the deceased, ideally, or your own, if you feel he could be of comfort to you), should be contacted. If you do not know the deceased's doctor, or cannot find the number, ring the local police station (Directory Enquiries will provide the number). The police will be able to give you the name and number of a local doctor. If there are any suspicious circumstances the police *must* be informed.

If the deceased had expressed a wish to donate any organs for transplant, it is very important that the relevant hospital should be notified immediately. If you cannot face making the calls, ask a friend or the doctor to do so.

As soon as possible you should obtain a medical certificate of death, register the death and arrange the funeral. If you need to claim widow's benefit, funeral benefit or supplementary benefit, the sooner you contact the Department of Health and Social Security the sooner your money will come through.

Medical certificate of death

This is supplied by the doctor attending on the body of the deceased and is free of charge. If there are any suspicious circumstances surrounding the death it should be reported to a coroner. The doctor or police will advise you.

Registering the death

The medical certificate of death has to be sent or taken to the Registrar of Births, Deaths and Marriages within five days, in England and Wales, or within eight days in Scotland.

It is usual for the partner of the deceased to go to see the registrar, but if for some reason, perhaps physical or emotional, you are unable to go, the doctor can attach to the medical certificate the names of people who may act on your behalf. (Legally these people have to know enough about the deceased to be able to supply all necessary details for the register: see below.)

The death must be registered where it occurred, except in Scotland where it can be registered either where it occurred or in the area where the deceased lived. You can find out the name, address and telephone number of the local registrar from the doctor, funeral director, post office or the telephone directory.

Registries are often rather clinical places. You cannot make an appointment, so you must be prepared to wait in a queue. It is a good idea to take a friend with you for support.

The registrar will want to know your name; the date and place of the death of the deceased; and his or her full name, sex, date and place of birth, address and occupation. In Scotland he will also ask the time of death; whether the deceased was married; the full name and occupation of the spouse; the name and occupation of the deceased's father; the name and maiden surname of the mother; and whether the parents are alive or dead.

Remember to check that he has written down the correct details before you sign the register. The registrar will give you two free certificates: a certificate of disposal, which should be taken to the funeral directors (no funeral may be held without one, and it is unwise to make any funeral arrangements until you have this form) and a certificate of registration of death – a standard death certificate.

The registrar will also give you leaflets on benefits and a form dealing with procedure for wills.

The death certificate

On the back of the standard death certificate is Form BD8, which is needed to claim the death grant (at present practically worthless), and widow's benefit. You might need extra copies of this certificate for the grant of probate, private claims on life assurance, pension schemes and friendly societies, or for showing to your bank or mortgage company.

For certain statutory purposes, such as claiming from trustee savings banks, national savings banks, national savings certificates and premium bonds, you have to obtain a 'specific death certificate', which is issued by the registrar, but you have to pay for these. Likewise, extra copies of the standard death certificate have to be paid for (see Chapter 14). If you can find out beforehand how many death certificates you will need – your solicitor or accountant will know – it will save you a lot of effort later on. If you think you will need copies, but do not know how many, note down the number of the entry and the date, as it will simplify requests made later.

ARRANGING THE FUNERAL

First, contact a firm of funeral directors/undertakers. (Members of the National Association of Funeral Directors are bound by a code of practice, so it is worth going to one of these.) They will be very sympathetic and will assume total responsibility for all the arrangements, taking the strain and worry off you. Before making any arrangements they will need to see the disposal and medical certificates, and you must agree a fee for their services.

It is important to remember that undertaking is a business, so you should ideally approach more than one firm for an estimate. Ask a friend or relation to help you.

Charges vary enormously and if you have a limited sum to spend you must tell the undertakers. At the time of writing a funeral will cost from about £400 to £800, depending on what you have in mind. Normally funeral expenses are paid out of the estate, and your bank manager will usually lend you the money to pay the undertakers while you are awaiting probate (see Chapter 12).

Building societies, the Department of National Savings and Trustee Savings Banks will often pay out up to £1,500 just on seeing the death certificate, without waiting for probate. If you are very short of money and applying for supplementary benefit you will be able to get a lump sum, but you must tell the social security office *before* making the funeral arrangements.

If money is a problem, undertakers will usually wait a short time for their bill to be paid, but you should check just how soon they want to be paid.

Ascertain from the undertakers exactly what they will provide and do not let them push you into having more than you want. The fee for a simple burial will include a coffin, a hearse and one following car, the bearers' and the undertakers' services. Embalming, use of the undertakers' chapel, and church or crematorium fees will be extra.

The undertakers will tell you the various costs of the local churches, cemeteries and crematoriums. They will also ensure that all the appropriate official forms are completed at the right time and taken to the right people, and will pay the vicar, grave-digger, cemetary officials and so on. If desired they will send out details of the funeral to friends and family and cards thanking people for flowers, etc. afterwards.

The undertakers will arrange for the body to be laid out if it is to remain in the house, or will take it to the firm's own chapel of rest. Undertakers usually request permission to embalm the body (this is a means of temporary preservation, carried out because some people may wish to see the body before the funeral). If you do not want the body embalmed, remember to specify this.

DEATHS ABROAD

The procedure for deaths abroad is quite complicated, so it is worth getting in touch immediately with the nearest British Consul, as well as the local doctor and police.

You have to register the death according to the regulations of the country in which the death occurred. If the British Consul registers the death this will enable you to get certified copies of the entry of death from the General Registry Office in London. Otherwise there will be no official record of the death in Britain.

If you prefer you can arrange a local funeral, and thus avoid the expense of bringing the body back. If you wish to have the funeral in England you will need a certificate of death (you must also obtain an authentic translation if necessary), or an authorization from the coroner in that country.

You will also need a 'Certificate of No Liability to Register' from the registrar of the district in which the body is to be buried or cremated. You will need to supply him with evidence, from the British Consul, that the death occurred abroad.

If you want a cremation you must also obtain a special certificate from the Home Office which provides dispensation for the otherwise necessary doctor's forms. You must send the documents which come with the body, application form for cremation and Certificate of No Liability to the Home Office, E4 Division, 50 Queen Anne's Gate, London, SW1H 9AT (tel. 01-213 7006).

A funeral director in Britain can be instructed to sort out the formalities and bring the body back for a funeral in the UK.

Funerals abroad
If the deceased died in England or Wales and is going to be buried or cremated in another country, ask the registrar to give you the appropriate form, and the address of the relevant coroner to whom it should be sent. You may not move the body for four days, unless the coroner directs otherwise. Your undertaker will then be able to make the travelling arrangements.

There are no restrictions on sending cremated remains out of Britain, although there could be restrictions at the other end.

CHURCHYARD BURIAL
Some people reserve and pay for a particular grave or burial site while they are alive. If you are not sure whether this is the case, check the deceased's will or other relevant documents. If no grave has been reserved, the deceased is entitled to be buried in the parish where he or she lived, but the burial fee does not entitle you to the right to choose the site of the grave. That decision rests with the minister.

Charges for burial vary (see Chapter 14).

CEMETERY BURIAL
If you do not want the deceased to be buried in a churchyard, the burial can take place in a cemetery run by the council or local authority. Most cemeteries are non-denominational. All local authority cemeteries have a section consecrated by the Church of England, and some have ground reserved for other specific religious denomina-

tions. Their fees vary, and are set by the owners, according to whether the services of clergymen are included, the type and size of grave, and so on. In cemeteries you can buy the right of burial in a particular plot, usually for 50 or 75 years.

CREMATION

The majority of crematoria are run by local authorities. A cremation may not take place before the cause of death has been absolutely ascertained. Four forms (see below) have to be completed prior to cremation, and if a coroner is involved you must tell him immediately whether you want a cremation. The forms can be obtained from the crematorium or from the undertakers.

Form A has to be completed by the next of kin and countersigned by a householder who knows you personally. Form B has to be completed by the doctor who attended the deceased before his death, and he has to see the body before he can sign. Form C is completed by another doctor who has practised in the UK for at least five years, is not a relative of the deceased or connected with the first doctor, and who also has to see the body.

Both these doctors will expect to be paid a nominal fee and they may also charge travelling expenses. Form F has to be signed by yet another doctor – the medical referee of the crematorium. These forms must be supplied to the crematorium at least 24 hours before the funeral, and the fees paid in advance (these cover the services of the medical referee, the use of the chapel, music, etc.). Arrangements for a clergyman to take a service at a crematorium are usually made by the deceased's partner or the undertaker. The ashes may be scattered or buried according to the partner's own wishes, or the wishes of the deceased.

RELIGIOUS CEREMONIES

If the deceased was religious and you want to have a religious ceremony, you should obviously go to see a minister of his or her denomination, who will advise and help you.

Outlines of the procedures for standard Anglican (Church of England), Roman Catholic and Jewish funerals are given below, followed by a few brief descriptions of specific rituals for other religions. All are subject to wide variation.

Anglican ceremonies

After the death and after a doctor has seen the body, the undertakers will take away the body to their Chapel of Rest, where it will be laid out, and, if desired, embalmed. It is normally possible to see the body at the chapel before the funeral.

You can arrange either for the undertakers to collect you with the coffin from your home, or for the procession to the church to start from the Chapel of Rest. At the church the minister always precedes the coffin, whether it is taken in before the mourners arrive or afterwards. This is a matter for you to decide on with the undertakers. The coffin is placed in front of the altar.

(If you are worried about walking into a crowded church with everyone looking at you, it might be better to ensure you are inside the church before the mourners arrive; alternatively, ask the minister if you can enter through a side door.)

The service usually lasts about half an hour. You may have hymns or not, as you wish, and it is usual for the minister or a good friend to say a few words on behalf of the deceased.

The coffin will then be carried out, followed by the mourners, and taken to the graveside. A prayer of committal (committing the body to the ground and to the hereafter) is said as the body is lowered into the ground, and the next of kin may throw a handful of earth or a flower into the grave. The mourners may then file past the grave if they wish.

In the case of cremation, the service may be held at a church beforehand, with the words of committal being spoken at the crematorium; alternatively, the whole service may be held at the crematorium. The coffin will be taken by the undertakers into the crematorium chapel, preceded by the minister, and laid on a catafalque (raised platform). The mourners will follow behind the coffin.

After the service, the prayer of committal is spoken as the coffin moves through a curtain into the committal room, out of sight. You can arrange to leave the room before this happens, or for all the mourners to leave.

If desired, two people are normally allowed to be present at the actual cremation. One to one-and-a-half hours later the ashes will be collected for you to scatter or keep as you wish, or as the deceased wished. The crematorium will send them on to you if you prefer.

Roman Catholic ceremonies

After the death the deceased's priest should be called and a few prayers will be said with the deceased's close family present.

Orthodox Roman Catholics are always buried. Although the Pope has decreed that Catholics may now be cremated, this tends to be done only by the less orthodox.

The procedure for a cremation is similar to that for an Anglican one, except that the body may be taken to the church and placed in front of the altar the evening before if a service in church is to precede the transfer to the crematorium.

In the case of burial, the body is taken to the undertakers' Chapel of Rest, where it is laid out. The coffin is usually received into the church the evening before the funeral, when the priest leads the procession into the church, followed by the undertakers with the coffin and then the mourners. The purpose of the service, which is short, is to dedicate the deceased to God. The service is normally attended by family and close friends.

The body is left overnight in the church before the altar. The following morning Requiem Mass is celebrated, taking about half an hour. The priest will say a few words about the deceased in his homily. There can be hymns, or not, as you wish. After the Mass there is an Absolution. The body is then taken to the grave, where more prayers are said, and the next of kin will sprinkle holy water over the coffin as it is being lowered into the grave.

Jewish ceremonies

Orthodox Jews are always buried.

After the death the body must not be left alone. The closest members of the family to the deceased are immediately released from all other duties and responsibilities. These are taken over by friends and by the local community.

The ritual washing of the body is done either at home by the family or by the Holy Association at a special building at the cemetery. The body is washed with warm water and dressed in a simple white shift. A candle is kept burning continually. The body must be buried as soon as possible after the death, and the coffin must be of plain, unpolished boards with rope handles, with no metal on it at all.

If the body has not been left at home the coffin will be taken past the deceased's home on the way to the funeral. The first part of the service takes place in the hall, where prayers are said. Close family members must wear old clothes, and the rabbi will cut and tear a piece of their clothing to show they are in mourning.

The coffin is then taken to the grave, halting several times for psalms to be sung. A short prayer is said by all the mourners as it is lowered into the grave and each member of the immediate family throws three handfuls of earth into the grave. The mourners then return to the hall, where more prayers are recited.

Immediately after the funeral the close family returns to the deceased's home to sit Shivah. This means sitting on hard, low stools while a ritual breakfast of hard-boiled egg, hard roll and a piece of salt fish is served, by other members of the family. In the evening prayers are said. The family continues to sit Shivah for seven days, during which time prayers are held three times a day and the family must not wash, shave, change their clothes or work. All menial duties are carried out for the family so that those closest to the deceased may concentrate on mourning.

Buddhists

The bodies are usually cremated, but there is no fixed ceremony. Before the cremation monks chant a text on the impermanence of the body, and afterwards everyone present prays for the deceased's happiness in his new life. Water is poured from two vessels as a symbolic gesture to dispel any evil which may surround the body.

Jehovah's Witnesses

Bodies may be buried or cremated. The service is very simple, either at a Kingdom Hall or at a crematorium. The elders say a few words about the deceased or read from the Bible, and a simple prayer is said over the graveside.

Greek and Turkish Orthodox

Bodies are always buried. The service is similar to a High Anglican service.

Hindus
Bodies are always cremated, and the funeral procession starts from the home. Often the coffin is filled with edibles – such as bananas and coconuts. There is often a long and complicated ceremony, with sacramental rituals. The family and friends usually insist on witnessing the actual cremation of the body.

Methodists
Bodies may be either buried or cremated. The service is very similar to an Anglican one, except that often several of the family and friends will say a few words on behalf of the deceased.

Muslims
Bodies are usually buried, after being washed and wrapped in three shrouds of differing lengths. Prayers are recited at a mosque before the body is taken to the cemetery, sometimes via the deceased's home. The body is buried with the right shoulder facing the east.

Quakers
Bodies may be buried or cremated. The service is a silent gathering, at which members of the congregation just speak when they wish to say something. The registering officer of the meeting conducts the ceremony following the civil laws on burial.

Russian Orthodox
Bodies may be buried or cremated. The service is similar to a Catholic service, except that the coffin is left open in the church. A ribbon is tied across the deceased's forehead, and every member of the congregation has to kiss the ribbon.

Salvation Army
Bodies may be either buried or cremated, and services are similar to Anglican ones. They are normally conducted by a Salvation Army elder in one of its halls.

Sikhs
The body is washed and dressed by the family in the funeral directors' premises, and is usually cremated. The

coffin may be taken to the home for prayers, and then on to the crematorium, where a service is held. Mourners file past the open coffin, either at home or at the crematorium.

Humanists
If you or the deceased are of no religious persuasion, but you wish to have a ceremony, the British Humanist Association, of 13 Prince of Wales Terrace, London W8, should be able to send someone to officiate at a humanist funeral ceremony; failing this, it will supply a booklet outlining the procedure to be followed. Non-religious ceremonies may be held at the graveside at most cemeteries.

NOTICES
Most newspapers will accept the text by phone and usually insist on a standard form of announcement, so you do not have to worry about how to word it. If you do not want to receive letters or flowers, or if you would like money donated to a particular charity, you should remember specify accordingly.

AFTER THE FUNERAL
If you want to book a local hotel or restaurant the undertakers can also look after this for you.

On the other hand, you may wish to be alone or have some friends back to your home. It is completely up to you and there is no need to follow convention. Some people find that having a full traditional funeral helps them and in some way, because it is so final, marks the beginning of their new life. Others would rather keep the occasion very quiet and low-key. You must do what you feel will be of most benefit to yourself.

Describing how she managed to cope with the funeral of her husband, one widow, Patricia, said: 'I arranged a very short service before the cremation of my husband, where a close friend read a few words and his favourite hymn was sung. I could not bear to be in the room when the coffin slid forward through the doors to be cremated, so I slipped out quickly. My friends and relations stayed, and I remember thinking to myself, "They must all think me very odd." Later on, when I could bear to talk about it, all my friends told me that they had thought I was very brave and sensible to do what I did. They said they would do the same when it came to their turn.'

Official papers and announcements
When the funeral is over and you can cope with it, you should return, cancel or alter all those personal documents such as passport, driving licence, car logbook, membership cards of clubs and associations, social security order books, medical card, pension or other benefit books, library books and tickets, etc., claiming where possible for unexpired membership subscriptions and so on. (See Chapter 13.)

After the funeral, or before if you have time and can face it, you must inform the Inland Revenue of the death (you could be entitled to a tax refund), the Department of Health and Social Security, the mortgage company (bank, building society, local authority), if applicable, and the relevant solicitors and accountants.

If there are life assurances or investments which have been taken out specifically for income benefit, for example, payments to be made to the deceased's children, inform the relevant companies. It is very easy to forget the existence of such policies; you might remember that there *is* such a policy, but not what it was for or with which company it was held. There might even be policies of which you are unaware. Your accountant may be able to help; otherwise, sooner or later you will have to go through all the papers of the deceased and see what comes to light.

This can sometimes be upsetting: you may, for example, come across correspondence you did not know about, or find out about something that had been kept from you.

If you still do not find any policies, check bank statements for standing orders, or study old cheque counterfoils.

You can obtain help and advice on financial, legal and practical matters from Cruse, the National Association for the Widowed and their Children, the Family Welfare Service and social services (see Chapter 13).

THE EXPERIENCE OF GRIEF
The grief you experience when your spouse dies is the most disabling of all emotions.

Death is still such a taboo subject that it is rarely discussed before the event, and when it occurs, especially if it happens suddenly, even those who might have thought they were prepared for it find themselves in a state of shock, quite ill-equipped to deal with the feelings that follow.

Although grief seems to be an almost unbearable burden at first, it must be remembered that it is also a healing process. Bereavement is akin to being physically wounded. For some time it is excruciatingly painful, but slowly the open wound closes, the pain recedes and you are left with a scar. As the years go by the scar fades.

Grieving is not something that happens; it is something that we do consciously. Through grieving, and thereby re-adjusting to our new life, re-assessing old assumptions and emotions, finding ourselves again, we emerge different, but, it is hoped, stronger and more complete individuals.

The stages of grief – first numbness, then anger, regret and loss – take time to work through. It can take one year, two, three or even more before these feelings diminish, but if you realize and understand that these stages are natural, that they have to be felt and understood, it will make them easier to bear. It will not make them go away, nor even lessen them, but they will not seem so alarming. Whether you are old or young, have been married for one or thirty-one years, the grief you feel has to be worked through in the same way. Although you may not experience these stages in any specific order, you will probably feel them all to a varying degree in time.

Sally, who had been happily married for 25 years when she lost her husband, showed me a diary she had been writing, cataloguing her feelings day by day after her husband's death.

For the first six months she did not feel anger at his death, regret or guilt; because he had suffered so badly for the last three years of his life, she had been almost happy for him to die.

For the following two months she suddenly felt anger that their happiness had been taken away, regret that having fought so hard together they did not win, and guilt that she was beginning to get over it and that the intensity of her feeling about her husband's death was diminishing.

One of the later entries read: 'I got over his death so well it seems weird to feel laid low by these feelings. But I suppose in time I'll conquer these as well.'

The important factor about working through grief is to realize that in the end you will be emotionally stronger than before. You will be the same person, but you will have developed and if you have fully understood your feelings and the reasons for them, you will have progressed emotionally.

Many widows and widowers have said that when they had come through their grief and were beginning to live a full life again, they felt they had acquired a better understanding and appreciation of other people. They wanted to know how they ticked and why they reacted in a certain way to particular situations. All of them stressed how grateful they were that some good had come out of their suffering.

UNDERSTANDING GRIEF

An understanding of grief will not prevent its intensity, its raw hurt, but it will make the burden lighter because you know that what you are feeling is not wrong. You must permit yourself to feel, to be able to express your feelings to yourself, to a friend, to your children, to the dog, to a blank wall.

Sometimes crying loudly is impossible if you are worried someone might hear. Perhaps you live in a block of flats or a terraced house where the walls are far from soundproof: remember, you can always sob to your heart's content with the radio turned up.

Elizabeth, a 50-year-old widow who had a house in the country and a flat in London, said, 'When I was in the flat and felt the need to cry my heart out in deep, wracking sobs, I had to play my records at top volume before I could let them out. I was worried about what the neighbours thought. In my country home I could wail and rant as much as I wanted. But in both places I felt so much better after a good cry.'

Many people have difficulty in working through their grief because they are frightened of their feelings, scared to accept that they can feel so intensely. If you repress these feelings, they will only come out later, possibly more viciously and at an unexpected time.

You cannot exorcise grief by making external changes in the hope that the internal feelings will go away. You may feel that by moving house, changing your hairstyle, or taking up evening classes with a vengeance, your grief will be overridden. These changes will solve nothing, even if they provide momentary distraction from the grieving process. There is nothing wrong in making changes when you are ready to make them, but irrational decisions made in haste will only cause you more problems later – which you could well do without.

Angus, who had been married for twenty-five years, said, 'I wish someone had told me not to make too many decisions too quickly. I went mad. I sold my wife's jewellery, sold the car, then bought another one which was a dud, moved house before I was capable of making a sensible decision and had to sell it again a year later to move to the place I really wanted to be, rather than somewhere I had thought, in a moment's rashness, I fancied.'

Dorothy was saved from making a bad mistake by an understanding salesman: 'A few days after my husband's death, I rang the salesman who had sold us the new car very recently and asked him to take it back. I could not drive at the time. He said he couldn't and urged me to let the matter ride for the time being. This I did, but only because I didn't know how to dispose of it. Thank God I did. After a few months I learned to drive, and am now so grateful I had a car I could use.'

ACCEPTING A NEW LIFE

Grief is nature's way of healing. The sadness may never leave you, but the ability to cope with and enjoy a new life will grow. You must come to terms with being on your own; it is now a fact of life. It may hurt, it may frighten, but you do no good by denying it to yourself. Of course, you are not really on your own. Many, many people have been bereaved. They have managed, and are managing. So can you.

Philip, who had been married for thirty years, said: 'I found a lot of comfort in that I was healthy and had lovely children. Knowing I am not the first, nor the last, to be left alone somehow helped.'

Another widower, Frank, said: 'My relief came when I suddenly realized that I was extremely grateful for and very lucky to have had all the happy times. And I stopped feeling sorry for myself because I was now on my own.'

Human beings are intrinsically selfish and grief, to a great extent, is a selfish emotion, albeit one we all experience at some time in life. It is right to grieve, but it is wrong to over-indulge in it.

Working through grief means accepting the situation and realizing that you are a person in your own right, not just half of someone else. You have to learn that people want to see you and love you – because of what you are, not what you are part of. Making a new friend who did not know your partner can be a giant step. Knowing that they will assess you and react to you because of how they see you and not because they are relating to your past can be very rewarding.

AVOIDING LONELINESS

Vanessa, a middle-aged widow with a grown-up son, admitted, looking back: 'I realized that I would have to suffer the grief but no one tells you about the loneliness.'

It is easy to give in to loneliness, to want to stay in isolation because you are scared of the outside world, scared of letting yourself back into it, or even enjoying it. You have to fight this, and at first it will be very difficult, but it can be done. By making small, gradual efforts you will find you can become part of society again, and in turn learn to appreciate being alone – which is *not* the same as being lonely.

You will have to re-assess yourself, and accept the facts you may have ignored before – perhaps because you felt it was not necessary in your relationship to face up to them, perhaps because your spouse did not allow you to. Now, you have the privilege of being able to make your own decisions about yourself, about what you want out of life and about life itself.

Everybody needs someone to talk to, to listen, to understand, to give confidence, to laugh with, to care. Most of us go through life using our friends as 'agony aunts' without necessarily realizing we are doing so, or talking to people about personal problems without actually asking for help.

It is only when a major problem occurs that we recognize and appreciate the help friends can give each other.

Many people find it extremely difficult to handle the emotions of others. They often feel the urge to suggest rather than support, to give their views on the matter –

what you should think, do and say – rather than realizing that *you* are the most important person at this moment and it is your views, not anyone else's, which are important, valid and in need of being understood and accepted.

Because they know that other people might not know what to do or say, people who grieve often feel they cannot show their feelings. If this is the case it must be up to the friend – if he or she can cope – to let that person know that they are prepared to support them and can handle their grief, that it is all right for them to 'let it all out'.

What people need at such times is a 'good mother', someone who will not crowd them or intrude, but will allow, indeed encourage, the person to work through their emotions.

Often a trained counsellor is the best person to turn to if you feel you cannot cope with your desperate lows, your anxieties, your depression, your guilt, your feelings of desolation and nothingness. Counsellors are trained in the skill of explaining matters non-judgementally. They are impartial and can advise without imposing their own per-sonal views. They may well be of more help than a friend or relation. (Details of counselling services are provided in Chapter 13.)

GUILT AND ANGER

A very common emotion suffered by bereaved people is guilt. Be prepared for feelings of guilt at things said or done, maybe just before your partner's death, maybe years previously. This is especially common when the death has been sudden, and you have not had time – whereas, with a long illness, you might have done – to apologize, say those little words of love you had been meaning to, or explain a misunderstood reaction.

Claire, who had been married for only two years, felt this very strongly when her young husband died of a heart attack: 'Not only was it unexpected, but he had been working away from home for a week. I felt guilt because I wanted to say so much I should have said before, and anger because he had left me before I could. I visited his body before the funeral and found this of enormous comfort. I spent quite a time with him, shouted at him for leaving me and for things he had done in the past, said the words I had wanted to say, expressed my love. I lifted his hand out of the coffin and held it. When I left the body, having given him a final kiss, a flood of relief and a feeling of peace engulfed me.

'I'm sure people think I'm mad for talking to a dead person, but I felt he could hear, could understand, and that was so important. I no longer feel that words have been left unsaid.

'A close friend said to me later, "I couldn't have done that, but I admire you for your courage and strength." I don't know where I found it, but I'm so glad I did.'

It is not unusual suddenly to feel great anger for something that your spouse may have done many years ago. If you look hard at that feeling you will find that you are feeling it now because at the time you did not let your anger through. This again is part of the grieving process: working through not only present feelings but many which may have been put aside in the past.

FREEDOM TO RUN YOUR LIFE AS *YOU* WANT

You may have been very happy with your partner, content with your life and lifestyle, yet there will undoubtedly have been things with which you were not completely happy, which you put up with for the sake of convenience, habit or your spouse's wish. Now you have the chance to work out exactly what you do want, and to become once more a fulfilled and peaceful person.

You will probably find that at first when you are on your own, you will keep up old rituals – turning on the television at the same time, watching programmes you do not really enjoy, going to bed at the same time – just out of habit. As you progress on your road to recovery, you will find that suddenly you have the strength to alter those habits you do not like and keep the ones you enjoy. That is a great step forward: it will mean you are starting to assert your own identity and have realized that you do not have to hang on to the past. Of course, habits and routines should not be changed just for the sake of it, or to show the world your strength or individuality; change them because you want to.

Many people find they do not want to sleep in the same bed, but do so at first because it was their bed when they were a couple and they can almost believe their partner will come back. A few weeks after losing his wife, John bought himself a new double bed. On the first night, although he still felt profoundly lonely, he also felt a sense of relief. It was his bed, and he was on his own. This was a step towards John's acceptance of his new life. A few weeks' later he positively enjoyed the knowledge that he could stretch, move, get up or put the light on without feeling guilty. He was worried at first about feeling good about it, but there was no reason for him not to. The person he loved was not there, and would never be there again. There might well be another person in the future with whom he will share his bed; meanwhile, he is right to enjoy the luxury of having it to himself.

On the other hand, there is nothing wrong in keeping the same bed as long as you are not conning yourself, wallowing in self-pity, using it to hide from the world or as an excuse to keep other people out of your life.

GOOD TIMES, BAD TIMES

There will be times of the day or the week which will be far harder to bear than others: evenings perhaps, when you come home from work; coming back to an empty house after a day out; or maybe waking up in the mornings.

Often, living a similar routine will remind you that your partner is not there any more. By altering it, you put your brain into a different cycle, one which does not encourage memories. For example, if you always made breakfast at 8.00 am, continuing to do so could be acting as a reminder of your loss. Perhaps you should have breakfast at a different time, or in a different room, or even have it at a café on the way to work.

Weekends, if you do not have a family, are always a hard time. Friends and families want to be together then, and are less likely to want anyone else around. Try to arrange outings in advance for these times; take up a hobby which you can do at the weekend, or a part-time job. Or perhaps you could take a course to which you can devote time during these two days. Make active provision for the way you will spend each weekend.

Jennifer, who had been married for 30 years when she was widowed, said: 'It is a mistake to do things you have been doing all your life. You must change your routine. I went on stocking the deep-freeze for months, although there was much too much food for me. I bought wine from the local wine merchant for nearly a year – because we had always done so – but never drank it. I would pour out a drink every night, as we had always done, but would often find it untouched the next morning.

'Because I lived in London in the week, and went up to the country where my husband was every weekend, after his death I found myself still hurtling up to Leicestershire on Friday night. I had no need to rush up the motorway like that, but it had become a habit. I am amazed I didn't write myself off. After a few weeks I realized what I was doing and managed either to go up on the Saturday morning, or to take it easier. It was so difficult remembering that there was no hurry.'

Anniversaries of the death will, of course, be excruciatingly difficult. But you will probably find that after the anniversary is over the depression disappears fairly fast – depending, of course, on how you are feeling generally. Birthdays, Easter, Christmas, bank holidays are all reminders, and you must be prepared for sudden relapses into grief after you thought you had come to terms with it. If this does happen, let the sadness come through, for if you are coping it will not last long.

Joscelyn Richards, principal psychologist for the National Health Service, comments: 'Until you have gone through the anniversary of a death, you are not really ready to get over it. It can take two anniversaries to rid you of the intense grief. On anniversaries for years to come you will always feel low, more vulnerable at that time, sometimes without actually realizing why, but the rawness of the grief will be alleviated after a period of time.'

Her views are borne out by most bereaved people. Amy, who was widowed after 30 years of happy marriage, said: 'Christmas alone was awful. I did the same things two years later as I had done when married. I bought champagne, but decided not to open it, cooked a duck and laid the table for one. It took me two days to open the presents, and I hardly touched the meal. I now take myself off to a hotel if no one else can have me. At least there are people there, and I am forced to make an effort, to cope and to try to be cheerful.'

This idea might not suit everyone, but at least it is a solution – and who knows whom Amy could meet!

BENEFITING FROM GRIEF

Grieving is a healing process, and although it seems difficult at the time to think that you might benefit through someone's death, it is true that you can. Working through your grief and gaining knowledge about yourself will eventually free you from the past (which should not be forgotten, but treasured and remembered with joy), and help you build a new life, as complete and fulfilled as before.

Look at it this way: how would you like people to feel after your own death? You might like to be briefly mourned. You would probably like people to think of you and not forget you, but you would not like people to be unhappy. And if, through natural grief, they were, wouldn't you be pleased if they could benefit from the experience and be able to be happy again?

CHAPTER 3

Separation and divorce

When you are newly separated or divorced you will feel shock, disbelief, loneliness, anger, bitterness, resentment, recrimination and rejection.

You may also hope that you might get together with your partner again, and although you know in your heart of hearts that this is unlikely, if you are the injured party you might live on this belief for months, or even years.

There is always an outside chance that this might happen, and even work out happily; it does in a few cases. But it is much more likely to be the case, whatever the cause of the rift, that there is no going back. Only by looking at yourself and your partner rationally, which is not easy if you have just broken up, will you know if anything can be retrieved. A depressing number of people damage their future lives by hanging on to futile hope.

Marjorie, 35, recalled her situation: 'I had been separated from my husband for five years. I knew during that time that he was living happily with another woman. But I still could not bring myself to believe that the marriage was all over. When the divorce papers finally came through it was an enormous shock. I reacted as if I never knew anything was wrong.'

When someone is widowed they know that what has happened is final. In some ways this can make the loss easier to bear. For anyone separated or divorced it can be harder to acknowledge, particularly as there are often elements of the past continuing into the future – children, maintenance, joint property, etc. – that demand the continuation of the relationship on some level, however minor.

If you have been deserted, you may be bitter and resentful. How *could* your partner who once loved you leave you now? What about all those years you have wasted, giving him or her all your love, care and affection? The thing to remember, if you feel like this, is that at least you do not have to waste any *more* time.

If you have children, you may be finding it hard to come to terms with letting them see a partner whom *you* never want to see again, but you must realize that to your children he or she is still a parent.

BLAMING YOUR PARTNER

A lot of separated or divorced people feel it might have been easier if their partner had died, because there are accepted ways in which a widow/widower is expected to behave. No one thinks it is his or her fault and everyone has a lot of sympathy and understanding.

In a divorce, blame is often apportioned to one side or the other, often unfairly and without proper understanding of the situation. You may feel people should be sympathizing with you when they are not. You could be eaten up with anger by what your partner has done to you.

Sometimes it is easier to come to terms with desertion if there is a positive reason – such as a new lover. If your partner has left you just because he or she did not want to live with you any more, you do not even have the satisfaction of blaming the break-up on somebody else.

Blame and resentment, however you have been treated, are a total waste of your emotions and your time. They are evil forces, and will gnaw away at your whole being if you let them. There is no reason to encourage them. Everyone feels these emotions at times, but that is no excuse to indulge them, and they should be fought against with all the strength you can muster.

Widows are usually in shock after the death of a husband. They feel as if everything is unreal, that they are looking down on themselves from afar; they are unable to concentrate. They will probably have to ask for help immediately concerning the funeral, the will or money matters. And for them there are people who can provide very positive practical help.

But divorcees are not in the same situation. There are no set answers as to how the money will be sorted out, how the house will be divided, who will have the children, and so on. Quite often friends are not sure what to say, what or whether to advise; there are feelings of conflict – whom to side with, whom to see – and the divorcee tends to be left high and dry when help is most needed. If you walked out on your partner, then perhaps you are feeling guilty, or even having to put up with reproaches from others because you 'deserted your partner' or 'made your children suffer'.

Mary, who was suddenly left on her own with two children, recalls: 'Many times I felt that I would have preferred widowhood to being a divorcee. It seems much more honourable. People can be quick to say or think "there must have been a reason why he left".'

And John, who had been married for twelve years and had two children under ten, said, 'My most difficult problem was the guilt feelings associated with what might appear to my children to be my deserting them, and the fear of us growing apart.'

A DIFFERENT KIND OF HURTING

Many people who separate or get divorced have suffered just as much loneliness or unhappiness during their marriage as they experience after. Belinda, a middle-aged woman married for the second time, had been aware before her husband walked out on her that something was going very wrong.

'When I got home after going to my daughter's speech day at boarding school to find a note on the kitchen table from my husband saying he had left me, it was almost a relief. I had had a year of intense unhappiness which had suddenly happened after 12 years of marriage and a very close relationship. So the loneliness had happened then and not when he actually left me. When someone suddenly becomes unapproachable, removes himself from you mentally, so that he is no longer somebody you know any more and becomes a stranger, the loneliness is very acute and I was certainly more unhappy then than when he physically left the house.

'Of course there is another kind of loneliness, too, when you are living alone. The noises you have become used to – when he arrives home, the noises in the bathroom morning and evening when he gets up and before he comes to bed, the shower, doors opening and shutting, and the ordinary routine of day-to-day living suddenly coming to an end. Not having anyone to tell when something important or unimportant occurs. A startling newsflash on television or radio or piece of information in the daily papers has to be digested alone. Even food becomes uninteresting.'

When you are alone, feelings you have been suppressing

for many years often rear their ugly heads. You may think now how you hated the way your partner ate his food; the way your mother was treated; that much-loved blue shirt. All the things which at the time you said nothing about, because they would only cause arguments, or did not seem that important, come to the fore. When this happens you must allow yourself to feel them, to work through them and learn to understand and accept them.

Even if you wanted the divorce, you may well suddenly find that you cared for your partner more than you thought, although you had convinced yourself that you hated him or her. Often it is because your subconscious mind has tricked your conscious mind into remembering all the bad times whilst forgetting the good.

Maybe hating made it easier for you to get through the separation and divorce, but there will always be a little bit of yourself which is attached to that person. Even if you do not want to acknowledge them, those feelings will eventually surface, if not emotionally, then physically. You might find yourself being unable to sleep, becoming irritable, tired, suffering from colds and headaches more than you usually do. You must be prepared for this, and to recognize that even years afterwards you *will* still feel something for your ex-partner.

GUILT THAT DIES HARD

Another difficulty that has to be overcome, if you have been the one to leave and have taken the children, is coming to terms with the fact that you have deprived your partner of the children and the children of one of their parents. In the midst of your own confusion, you also have to sort out the children's emotions.

Heather, who had been married for seven years and had two young children, looked back on her own experience eighteen months after separating: 'I wanted to leave my husband, but I felt desperate about depriving him of his children, and the children of him. I had wanted to leave for two years, but could not because of the children. Eventually I came to the conclusion that it was better for the children to have a happy home life with one parent than an unhappy one with two. Thankfully my husband and I have stayed on good terms so he can see them as much as he wants. But I find it so painful every time he says goodbye to the children, seeing the look of desperation and unhappiness on his face, because he knows I have the children and he does not. It still cuts me up terribly.

'We told the eldest boy, who was six, together. We explained we would not be living together any more, but that this was nothing to do with him. We told him we loved both our children very much, but although we liked each other we did not love each other any more, so we could not live together. He cried when we told him, but he is OK now.

'He told his teachers what had happened, but they did not believe him at first, because they saw me and my husband together. As soon as I realized this, I explained the situation to them, and after that they were very good. They asked me if I wanted them to do anything special for my son, but I thought it would be best if they treated him as they had always done.

'My daughter was only three, so she did not understand. She misses her father when he is not there, but seems to cope with it.'

Perhaps you also have the problem of coping with the knowledge that your ex-partner is having a marvellous time with somebody else, and acknowledging the possibility that your children may become attached to their new 'parent'. All those doubts and insecurities you may have felt over the years – you are not pretty, you are unlovable, you are impossible to live with – come into your mind. You remember the hard words your partner might have spoken and wonder if they are true. Even innocent remarks made by your children begin to prey on your mind.

RE-BUILDING SELF-CONFIDENCE
You might blame yourself for the split-up, but always remember partnerships and break-ups are not one-sided. Two people with equal responsibility are involved.

Veronica, a middle-aged divorcee, felt this strongly. 'My worst emotional problem,' she admitted, 'was the realization of my inadequacy to repair a relationship.'

Fred, 41, also felt 'a certain inadequacy . . . a lack of confidence that I can ever again cope with living with another person. I always thought I was reasonably easy-going, but my marriage made me wonder whether I really am somewhat irritable and difficult to live with. By flinging myself quickly into purely sexual relationships, I managed to recover some of that confidence. At least I felt: I might be over 40, but there are still people around who find me attractive, and like my company.'

And Paul, 28, married for seven years, said: 'I found it hard to come to terms with the acceptance of defeat, that try as hard as one might, some things just will not work. I guess, in a word, it's one's pride.'

It is not easy to regain lost self-confidence, but look back at your past, even back to your childhood, and try to remember a time when you patched up an argument, made someone feel better, diffused a row. Give yourself evidence that you *are* able emotionally to achieve things.

Write down all the things you are good at – cooking or painting, being good with figures, or with children, and so on. Your face might not be beautiful, but what about your legs, your hair, your laugh, your singing voice? It will probably surprise you to find out how many good points you have. Once you learn to love yourself, to realize that there are two sides to a break-up, and not to put all the guilt and blame on to yourself, you will make yourself a more attractive and, if you have learnt anything, a more giving person.

There is bound to be some bitterness and recrimination between partners about what has happened. However hard it is, you must try to minimize these feelings. Do not catalogue the faults: seek and find the good points. No one is perfect and everyone needs understanding. Accept the situation and make sure mistakes are not repeated. You should try to adopt a logical approach to the past, and recognize the good and bad in both of you. If your ex-partner is being unreasonable, or stupid, or still playing games, you do not have to join in. If at last you have got your mind and life sorted out, explain this. If he or she will not listen, never mind – you have done your best.

STARTING AGAIN WITH SOMEONE ELSE

You may be very reluctant to get involved with another person, because you have been hurt once and do not want to put yourself in a vulnerable position again. But if you have grown, emotionally, as a result of the break-up, discovered things about yourself that you perhaps ignored before, learnt what you really like and dislike, want and do not want, you will be less likely to make the same mistake again.

Susan, divorced for two years, reflected on her own situation: 'I am much more self-contained and self-reliant. At first I was totally lacking in self-confidence, but that has got better. Now I feel a strength in knowing I have been to the depths of depression and back. I won't worry if things get depressing again, because I know I will recover.'

Mike, 33, married for ten years, spoke in similar terms: 'I was devastated when my wife asked me for a divorce, but I kept the traditional stiff upper lip, and all my friends and workmates seemed to assume that I was coping OK. Secretly, I wasn't. When I was left alone at work, I used to burst into tears, and didn't dare tell anyone, because I thought they would laugh at me.'

'Having been to a counsellor, suggested by my doctor, I slowly sorted myself out. And having been to the depths and back again, to my surprise I am actually helping a colleague at work who is going through the same thing, and I feel really good.'

There is a lot of comfort in such testimonies. Having been to 'the depths' of depair and survived, you will know, through experience, that if you ever have to face despair again you will come out the other side. And when all seems black you will know that in the distance a light beckons.

Many divorcees have spoken of becoming 'a new person'. One of them, Marian, said: 'I have changed since my divorce, I have learnt to assess people better and to fend for myself. I haven't much money but at least I know where I am going.'

Another, Wendy, divorced with two children, reflected: 'I have matured, become more independent. Also to a certain extent I have become more self-centred. I am now more satisfied with my life and myself, and have become very ambitious.'

Even a woman who had been through a very violent marriage, and had eventually found the courage to leave her husband, said: 'I am single because I choose to be. I know that no man will hit or hurt me again. I have a choice now, which I was denied before. I am me, not anybody else. I have made mistakes, but I am me at last.'

Tracy, separated for 11 years and divorced for eight, said: 'I can cope better with life, and have learnt a lot about what makes people tick. I am more easy-going, far more with it. Everyone comes to me with their problems and I can help them. I don't cry as much, and am harder and far more cynical.'

Lyn had also gained in self-confidence: 'To quote a cliché, I have discovered myself. I don't think I am anything like the person my husband left. Without wishing to be big-headed, looking back I think I've coped very well and I don't fear change or challenges as much as before.'

THE MALE PREDICAMENT

Although a man is usually in a better financial situation, unless he is paying heavy maintenance, divorce is frequently more difficult for him because society expects him to be strong, and to recover fast. Absurdly, going to a counsellor or doctor for help is considered – by ignorant people – to be a sign of weakness, which nobody should admit to. This applies to women as well, but sadly the attitude is far more entrenched where men are concerned.

James, divorced after sixteen years of marriage, described his feelings: 'I felt down and rejected. It was the first time I had felt so low in my life. I found it difficult learning to cope on my own, and shopping for just myself. No one seemed to realize the difficulty I was having, and I found it impossible to ask women friends for their advice.'

Walter, 38, married for six years, echoed the sentiments of many divorced fathers: 'I desperately miss my children, being woken up early in the morning, asked to play football. I also miss the family unit, going out together, visiting people together.'

It is easy to forget that when men with children divorce they lose not only their wife, and quite often their home, but also their children.

DIVORCE AND MORALITY

Another problem, unique to the situations of separation and divorce, is the underlying moral aspect. You may find it very hard to come to terms with that fact that you vowed in church 'to love and to cherish till death us do part'.

If this becomes a major problem, visit a counsellor or a clergyman (Chapter 13 lists counselling services). Counsellors can help you sort out your thoughts and emotions. For example, you may well be confused by what your parents or society instilled into you about the sanctity of marriage and your own spiritual doubts. Forgiving others is a generous, but often easy, gesture; forgiving yourself is harder, but just as rewarding.

Clergymen can also help. You do not need to be religious to approach a priest with your problems. Some encourage you to make the marriage work, but nowadays many have a far more tolerant attitude towards divorce. If nothing else, most will at least be helpful and understanding, and will listen objectively to your problems. Many will be able to help you to come to terms with them and put your mind at rest. If you *are* religious, do try to discuss your situation with your local minister of religion. Even the Catholic Church now recognizes that if there is no chance of reconciliation, a fresh start (in a legal and civil sense) is preferable to the partners' remaining in misery for the rest of their lives.

INDEPENDENCE
Value and appreciate your new-found independence. Do not be frightened of it. Work on it, enjoy it and when the time is right for you to start another partnership, let your independence hold you in good stead. But beware of becoming too independent. Being confident and strong does not mean being selfish, but being able to give and take with equal joy.

It may take some time for you to become happy with yourself in your new situation. As Paul, 36, on his second divorce, said: 'I feel that people in situations [similar to mine] must accept that life will not settle down until a considerable time has elapsed – conservatively, 18 months to two years – and also that one's own personality can and often does change during that time. It is as if one's inner consciousness embarks on a house-cleaning process, reorganizing and sprucing things up. But it does leave one less inclined to allow the furniture to be moved around in one's absence.'

When there has been a separation, try not to assess it in terms of blame. Work out with yourself, or with a friend or counsellor, what you might have been able to do to help your marriage, or what you expected from your partner that he or she was unable to give. Accept that you are not perfect, your partner was not perfect, but that to live together with someone there has to be give and take and no one person has the right to do all the giving or the taking. And before you embark on another relationship give yourself time to find yourself, love yourself and know yourself.

Diana talked of her experiences in terms of respect: 'I needed time to get myself together after our separation. . . I lost my self-respect through being married, and lost others' respect by separating, but after one year I had regained my self-respect. Now I feel I am ready to give to someone else again.'

If you need help in sorting out your own emotional problems, or in working out the best and most civilized way to divorce, with regard to yourself and your children, there are several counselling and conciliation services which can help.

Conciliation does not mean reconciliation. Conciliation services are intended to help couples sort out their divorce, with special regard to children, in the most sensible and caring way, and to avoid hurt, bitterness and recrimination by involving a neutral third party, while counselling services will help you work out your emotional problems both before and after a separation, or divorce. You can attend on your own, with your partner, or with your children.

CHAPTER 4

Loneliness

Loneliness is a part of many people's lives, but for anyone who has become single it is a particular problem. With some, loneliness seems to last for a lifetime; with others, it comes and goes. It can vary in intensity from desperation to an occasional bout of weeping.

There are, of course, people who choose to be on their own and who positively enjoy their solitude. For them, loneliness is not a problem.

Others suffer desolation when they are completely alone. They want desperately to be with someone, to meet and mix with people; they need to speak to someone so badly that they will do anything to achieve this. For example, Caroline, a young divorcee, admitted: 'I used to go out to the local shop to buy a loaf of bread when I already had ten loaves in the deep-freeze – just to speak to another human being.'

But being alone is not the same as being lonely. Being alone can be welcome, a privilege that some people who would value it can never enjoy.

To begin thinking about being alone in a more positive light, remember, as the first step, that you are not unique. According to a recent survey 25 per cent of the British population defines itself as 'being lonely'. Of that number over 4 million people are widowed, divorced or separated. So if you were to stop for a minute to think about people other than yourself, to look outside your own world, you would find that out of every ten people you know at least two of them are in as much need of emotional human contact as you.

Looking outside yourself and being aware of other people's loneliness forces you to think about others and to realize that it is not only you who are alone. This exercise may seem obvious, but give it a try.

Secondly, do not rush things. Take small steps into

sociability. If you fling yourself into a room full of people, you will only terrify yourself and use this as an excuse not to go out again. When you are ready to, try visiting a friend or making contact with that person round the corner who might be just as lonely as yourself. By making someone else feel part of the human race, by letting that individual know that he or she is not alone, you will be helping yourself.

One-to-one relationships will be easier than dinner parties or large gatherings at first, and are a positive beginning.

Think of building your new life like a pyramid. Once you have built a solid base, the next layer can be laid. Each layer needs fewer and fewer blocks to complete, and is therefore easier.

Some people find it hard to admit to themselves that they are lonely, let alone to others. Yet there is nothing to be embarrassed about. There is nothing wrong with you. Loneliness is not a disease. People will not run away from you. It is imperative to talk about it, though not in a confessional way, nor in a self-congratulatory way, nor even in a self-indulgent way. Just admit that you are lonely and that you need people.

Some people are better at handling other people's loneliness than others. Some, maybe friends of yours, will not know how to cope with the situation. There will be other people who are more receptive, more understanding and more willing to help. More often than not, however, you will find you have to make the first move.

If you find it difficult to talk to people who knew your partner, whatever the circumstances of the loss or separation, remember that there are new people to meet who will enjoy your company on its own terms, not because of what you were or were part of. You may find that new contacts give you more than old friends.

This was certainly the experience of Pauline, a divorcee with a young child, who recalled: 'I actually found it a relief not to have to go on explaining to friends I knew, to start all over again with a clean slate. Most importantly I realized how vital it is to keep up contacts, and I will do that now if I marry again.'

Sheila, a middle-aged widow, found that she valued being seen not as a widow but simply as a colleague by people at work: 'I was so glad to get back to work, to people who would not continually ask me how I was, how I felt, whether I was feeling better. They let me get on with my life and I felt I could talk to them as a normal human being – which was hardly how I felt at the time, but I knew I had to be for my sanity.'

When you are feeling low you might be tempted to grudge the effort you have to make to be outgoing. It is easy to fall into the trap of believing that no one gives a damn, when in fact the opposite is true; if you let such feelings cause you to put off making an effort to relate to other people you will find yourself wallowing in destructive self-pity. You have to pull yourself out of it.

ACCEPTING WHO YOU ARE

One of the keys to overcoming loneliness is learning to accept yourself as a worthwhile person. That means the inner you: if you do not love yourself, how can you expect others to love you?

You have to come to terms with your new situation, to accept that it can never be the same as it was before. You are on your own, and you are going to make it better than before. Sitting back does no good. No magic fairy can conjure up hordes of caring people beating a path to your door.

A psychologist with considerable experience of lonely people said: 'Some patients come to me expecting me to make them instantly sociable, happy and outgoing. They believe I can prescribe some wonder drug or possibly hypnotize them into uncovering some key factor that will enable them to conquer the world. They are saying "Change me". I have to get the idea across that they have to do the work, which isn't always a welcome message.'

Dieting, changing the style or colour of your hair, buying a new wardrobe or moving house are only temporary diversions. They will not achieve anything by themselves, though they may contribute to some degree to making you happy with yourself.

Take a good look at yourself. Make a list of all the good things about you. Write them down. If you can only write down one thing you think is worthy, that is enough. You have that one thing to offer, and of course you are bound to have more: everybody has several good points.

VULNERABLE TIMES

Be aware that loneliness will come on you at your most vulnerable times, at night, at weekends, or at holiday times. If weekends are the worst times, try to plan for them. Take yourself off to see something or somewhere new to you – with a friend if possible. Or take a course, preferably one that brings you into contact with others, which will keep you busy at these times.

If you feel lonely at night, put the radio on. Go to bed earlier or later than you used to do, change your routine, read a book, a magazine, the papers. Take up a hobby you have not bothered with for years, do a jigsaw, or do a chore you have been putting off. Anything is better than sitting feeling miserable, remembering how things were, how things might have been. This is your new life: do not forget it can be a good one, even a better one, if you make the effort.

But do not make the mistake of thinking that by filling up your day with things to do and being busy you will necessarily combat loneliness. Fighting and winning the battle is learning to be alone *and enjoying it*. True acceptance will heighten your perceptions and enable you to make the most of your life.

Stella, a divorcee of 43, recalled that the effort she made took some time to reap benefits: 'When I was left on my own, I felt I never wanted to see anyone again. But I knew I had to start getting out and about again. I joined new clubs. In fact, I joined every club going. I starting knitting. I even learnt to drive. It was an effort. Sometimes I really had to talk myself into going out, not ringing up to say I was ill or giving some other excuse. Now I am glad I did all those things. I have stopped doing some of those hobbies, because I know I really didn't enjoy them all that much. But I have new friends now, new interests, and know that I am happy to be by myself when I am, and happier in myself altogether.'

PETS

One way of helping you feel less lonely is by having a pet. A cat, dog or even a bird can be a marvellous companion at the times when you are feeling most vulnerable. Although an animal can never take the place of human friendship, pets can help indirectly. They can make you feel a little more sure of yourself, and less unloved. It helps, too, to be responsible for some creature who depends on you absolutely for its food and lodging. And when you do get round to meeting other people, this will help you to project a more positive and therefore more attractive outlook.

GETTING OUT AND ABOUT
Going outside the home and meeting other people is essential, though it is not easy to begin. There are many possibilities. For example, you could join a club. There are social clubs and networks for one-parent families, widows, the divorced and separated, and homosexuals, which provide meeting places for people on their own, and a chance to talk to others in the same situation as yourself. They organize social evenings and days out, holidays and help with babysitting. (See listings in Chapter 13 for both this chapter, 4, and Chapter 9.)

If you do not like the idea of joining a crowd, you might be happier to meet others on a one-to-one basis. Computer dating services, and introduction/marriage/friendship bureaux which put compatible people in contact with each other can play a useful role at such times, as long as your initial expectations are not too high.

The advantage many people find in one-to-one meetings is that they do not have to contend with competition, a possible problem in, say, a club or party situation when you may go into a crowded room knowing no one. It is up to you – and the person you are meeting – to make a go of it. In a group situation, however, you may fear rejection more strongly, and fear being ignored, being made to feel inferior, or being shown up because you cannot make friends.

You are likely to be especially sensitive to such predicaments if you have just become single, whereas in meeting just one other person there is a 50 per cent chance that you will at least be able to forget your problems for a while. If it does not work, it will only be you and the other person who knows, and it will reflect badly on neither of you.

The marriage/friendship bureaux have different methods of working. Some insist on interviews with everyone concerned. They find out what sort of person you are, what sort of person you are looking for, then look through their books for a suitable match. Your particulars will be sent to that person, and theirs to you. Then it is up to one of you to make contact. The bureaux will usually help if you are worried about making the first move, and talk to you afterwards if you are not happy with what happened. Some people go to these agencies specifically looking for a marriage partner, others just for friendship; some use the bureaux' services for several years, meeting more and more people.

Other bureaux just provide contact names. They send out a list of hundreds, with little or nothing said about those people. Box numbers can be used to preserve confidentiality. However, some not-so-reputable companies will give out your name, address and telephone number to anyone who asks.

So if you decide to try a marriage or friendship bureau, find out exactly how it operates. Will the personal details you supply be treated in confidence? How much personal attention will you receive? Exactly what services will you be given for the fee charged?

Another possibility is computer dating, which is more impersonal but is likely to have the advantage of a large membership, and could therefore increase your chances of finding like-minded people.

You might think you could not possibly consider joining such an agency, for there is still something of a taboo clinging to them and a few have occasionally come into disrepute. However, they could be, as they have been for others, the answer to your need to meet people. You will find that those who use these services are *not* socially inadequate, but normal people who, perhaps because they have moved house, changed jobs or lost many of their past contacts through divorce or bereavement, wish to make new friends. They are not necessarily looking for a mate, but for a new social life with people who have similar interests.

Another avenue to consider is advertising. You could try putting an advertisement in the personal column of a newspaper or magazine, or reading other people's advertisements. Such a recourse will not appeal to everyone, but can be successful. Obviously you must be aware that some people who advertise and who respond to advertisements are cranks, but if you are prepared to persevere you might find what you are looking for. If you decide to advertise, word the advertisement carefully and beware of double meanings. When answering advertisements, talk to the advertiser several times on the phone before you agree to meet. Do not give anyone your address before you have met and assessed him or her, and make the first meeting at a public place, rather than at either home. It is always better to err on the side of caution.

Evening classes are an obvious possibility. You may think you are not interested in anything enough to want to learn about it. But think again, and think hard: the range of classes available is surprising, and surely few people could truthfully claim that there is absolutely nothing they would not like to learn more about. Classes will enable you to meet people with whom you have at least one mutual interest, which gives you a basis on which to build up friendships. Information about evening and other classes is available from public libraries (see also Chapter 13).

Working, if you are not already in employment, is something else to consider. You may have never worked, or might not have worked for some time, but you could always try taking up a temporary or part-time job to see how it goes. Not only will you meet people, but you will earn some handy extra cash. However, do be careful if you are receiving supplementary benefit, because you can lose your benefit if you earn over a certain amount. For further details see Chapters 12 and 7.

You might have a special talent which you enjoy, but which other people find dull – such as darning, mending shirts, putting up shelves or home decorating. If you have, you could put an advertisement in your local paper offering your services. There might well, for example, be a man on his own who has a pile of socks that need mending, or a woman who has managed to paper the hall but does not feel she can tackle the stairwell.

If you are not interested in money, why not do some good in your local community, where help is always needed? Whether it be seeing to the flowers in a hospital, looking after mentally or physically handicapped children, the sick or the elderly, such voluntary work is rewarding both for the people you are helping and for you, in terms of its emotional benefits: we all need to be needed. Local authorities and voluntary organizations will be able to supply you with details of who needs your help. (For names and addresses see Chapter 13 and Bibliography.)

A drama group could also provide you with a new interest. There is bound to be a local amateur group in your area. If you do not want to act you are likely to find yourself much in demand for work behind the scenes, maybe with costumes, lighting, props or scenery. You could easily find yourself becoming more involved than you ever expected.

If gardening is something you enjoy, that too could provide your route to new friendships. You may not have a garden of your own, especially if you have had to move. If this is the case, and you miss pottering around in the garden, remember that there are many people desperate for someone to do a bit of weeding or cut the grass and generally look after the garden. If this appeals, put an advertisement in the local paper, or a card in a local shop window: you will be surprised at just how many replies you get. Gardening can be therapeutic, and the fresh air and exercise will certainly not harm your health.

If you are an active person, or if you feel you should be more active than you are, you can join a sports club and play tennis, squash, badminton, football, or whatever. Take some lessons if you are new to the game or no good at it, and do not suppose that if you miss the ball, fall over or flatten the shuttlecock you will be thought stupid or inept. Everyone is a beginner initially, and you will probably meet many others at the same stage as you.

If you have a particular hobby you enjoy, find a club for it that brings together people with similar interests. The local newspaper or public library, or perhaps a specialist magazine, will put you in touch with one (see also Chapter 13). If you cannot find one, or cannot find one near enough, why not try starting one? Put an advertisement in your local paper or shop window, and if you get a few replies from like-minded people, suggest meeting every so often to see how it goes.

Getting out and doing one activity will lead to other interests and more friends. You only have to set the ball rolling. Try not to give up if something does not go right the first time; eventually things will begin to work for you.

CHILDREN

If you have children, the problem of loneliness might be less apparent at first, both to you and to outsiders.

Obviously children are company, but however much of your time they occupy you can still be as lonely as someone who is literally alone. You still need to learn to be alone without being lonely, and you may find it harder than others to cultivate new adult friendships.

If after becoming single you have had to put all your energies into looking after your children, and especially if they are young and demanding, you may have put aside your feelings of grief and loneliness because you have not had the time, energy or inclination to work through them. But sooner or later, when the children go to school, or leave home – a few months or a few years later – you will be left with not only an empty home, but an empty world. The shock of old feelings welling up so long after the event can make them seem much worse, and harder to deal with.

On the other hand, children can actually help you cope with both the pain – of bereavement, or of divorce – and loneliness, because you cannot give up on life if there are children around. Through their young friends you could extend your adult contacts, too, by cultivating your acquaintance with their parents.

SUICIDE

Sometimes loneliness seems too hard to bear, and at some stage it may cross your mind that life is not worth living. Many people experience such feelings when suffering from grief. You have to remember that although you have lost someone who was very dear to you that person was not everything in your life. You are still here, and there are other people who love you and want you around.

Even if you wish to ignore the religious and moral reasons for not taking your own life, think about the hurt your moment of desolation will cause your family, friends, colleagues and neighbours. Think about the doctors, nurses, ambulancemen and police who will have to become involved. These people are not just bureaucratic organizations, but caring human beings. People *do* care about you: your present grief will be experienced by them to some degree if you go through with your suicide. Is it fair to them?

Most people who attempt suicide do not mean to kill themselves. Often, it is a plea for help – and a selfish one, too. Just think about it for a second. If you want help you can get it. Go to your doctor, a counsellor, a priest or a friend. Talk to the Samaritans. There are people out there who can help you, and want to help. Think, too, of the many people who have felt like you but survived, either because they were dissuaded or because their attempt failed. How many of them, in time, have looked back and wished their lives had ended at their moment of despair? It would be difficult to find one. In the end, the old cliché about time being a great healer always proves infallible.

Trevor, 38, divorced after six years of marriage, bore this out. He recalled: 'Suicide did enter my head, although I consider it a coward's way out, and I really did not want to be a coward. But for the first time in my life I thought that it would make life easier for some . . . if I wasn't around. Then I remembered the people who would miss me, and my children, who had already suffered enough. I did not want them to suffer even more. Now that I am very happily remarried, it sends a shiver down my spine when I think what I nearly did!'

Denise, aged 49, and divorced, also mentioned that her child had been a deterrent to suicide: 'I felt I would never be able to cope on my own. I had never had to in the past, and I just didn't know where to start. My whole life was with my husband and my child, and he had left me for somebody else. I would lie there at night thinking, "Why do I bother to go on? Wouldn't it be easier to just give up?" But something inside me never let me go further than that thought. I couldn't have left my child alone, and deep down there was something in me saying, "Get up and fight. He's living on, why shouldn't I?" Now I realize things do change. I never thought I would enjoy independence, but I do now. There are many compensations – even little things like going to bed when you feel like it, and being able to go out or stay in as I want.'

Anne, 26, said: 'My boyfriend, whom I had been living with for seven years, left me and I was made redundant from a job I was really enjoying. They always say things come in threes, and two weeks later my flat-mate announced she was getting married, which meant I had to give up the flat. My world had caved in. I swallowed every pill I could find. The next thing I knew I was in hospital having my stomach pumped, feeling very sick and sorry for myself. The nurses were wonderful. I felt so guilty for wasting their time that I pulled myself together, found a job from the paper and a new flat. I will never forget their kindness.'

TURNING THE CORNER

However black things seem, your life can be made to work for you.

Mandy's story might give you some encouragement. Aged 53, she had been at a low ebb for some time after being widowed.

'I loved my husband dearly but he was very possessive, and he didn't like me having friends and interests of my own. As a result the friends we had were his. When he died I leaned heavily on my daughter, who was very supportive, but when she wasn't there I felt unbearably lonely. For some time I had read advice in magazines telling people to sit down, take stock and take action. But I had never done anything about it.

'A young neighbour came in for a cup of coffee and suddenly broke down. She poured her heart out about her husband leaving her. I found myself spouting out all the good advice I had been reading, but taken no notice of myself. She went away cheered up and vowing to do something about it. I suddenly thought it was about time I took my own advice.

'I listed the things that I thought were positive about myself. Not much, but it was a start, and it came home to me just how boring my life had become. The next day I went down to my local travel agent and told them I wanted to go on holiday where there would be people and it would be fun. To my surprise, I learnt that if you book a holiday at the last moment and don't care where you are going you can get incredible bargains.

'When I got home I wondered what I had done, but it was too late. I had a wonderful holiday and met several interesting people who have since become good friends. And when I returned, I didn't get back to my boring life. I joined clubs, went to evening classes to learn things I had been meaning to for years. I lost weight, and found that easier because I had more interests. Now I didn't have to eat for consolation and comfort.

'It was hard to start it off, but I can see now how worth while my efforts have been. Why didn't I do that long ago?'

As Mandy's confidence grew, so she became more interesting to other people. It is fairly obvious that if you have, and give off, a positive outlook people will react to you in a positive way. If you go round like the angel of doom, you cannot blame people for steering clear.

Each one of us has different ways of coping with our own crises. There is no such thing as a right way or a wrong way to deal with emotional or social problems, but however you handle it, it must feel right for you.

You will get out of life only what you put in. It is no good, for example, joining a singles group if you just attend but make no effort. If you want to gain something from that group, you must be prepared to contribute.

In our modern world just surviving can be hard work. It is doubly hard to pull yourself out of an emotional trough, but it is not impossible. And once you have done it you will be stronger, better equipped to face life, and more able to help yourself and others.

THE LUXURY OF BEING ALONE

When you are part of a couple, the idea of getting some time to yourself is often a luxury of which you only dream. When you are suddenly single, being alone can turn into a nightmare. You can turn it back into a luxury by using the time and space to your own advantage. It can give you the chance to look at yourself objectively without interference from others, to learn about your feelings and understand your responses to other people. It can allow you time to work out what you *really* enjoy doing, and what you did before out of habit or convenience. If you understand yourself you have a better chance of understanding others, and you will bring a wiser, more positive attitude to any future relationship. You can learn to appreciate and enjoy solitude. Instead of being frightened, use this time to relax and recharge your batteries. Enjoy the luxury of being on your own. Next time you think 'I wish I wasn't alone', turn it round and think: 'I am lucky to be alone, and to have the ability to do exactly what I want, when I want.'

There may be a time in the future when you will want to give your time again to someone else. Meanwhile, make the best of being independent.

CHAPTER 5

Health

Health is your most valuable asset. To be healthy means you can cope more readily with external pressures and day-to-day worries, and are readier to take on new challenges.

Mental and physical health are interlinked and interdependent. When you are emotionally 'low', you are more vulnerable to disease because your natural defences are also run down.

STRESS

Researchers at the University of Washington have developed a scale showing the different levels of stress caused by various life-changes. Top of the list is the death of one's spouse at 100 points, followed next by divorce at 73 points and marital separation at 65. Moving house or having trouble with in-laws rates medium to low on the scale.

Stress affects us both mentally and physically. We feel tired, depressed, unable to cope with the simplest of household chores; on the physical side we suffer more from headaches, palpitations and ulcers and become susceptible to minor ailments, such as the common cold.

Research has shown that divorced, separated or widowed people are more likely to be ill than others. The fatality rate for such people, especially elderly widows, is also high. There are two possible reasons for this: first, that they are less able to cope with the stress than younger people; second, that they lose their will to live, succumb more easily to illness and fail to look after themselves as well as they might have done when their partner was alive.

DEPRESSION

If you are feeling low, do not be afraid to go to your doctor. It may well help just to talk to him. Nowadays you are not as likely to be given anti-depressants or tranquillizers as readily as was the case some years ago; your doctor will use his own judgement. If he really feels you will benefit from drugs, such as sleeping pills (sleep becomes even more important at times of stress), he will give you a small number of the mildest pills he thinks will work.

The doctor will decide whether or not tranquillizers or anti-depressants should be prescribed. Some prefer not to prescribe tranquillizers until a few weeks after their patient's loss; others will recommend anti-depressants later on if the patient is not pulling through. But they will explain to you that these drugs help only on a short-term basis. Long-term help must come from you in the form of understanding and coming to terms with your feelings, perhaps by talking about them to friends, relatives or counsellors.

Unfortunately many doctors do not have as much time as they would like to spend with their patients. Doctors in some localities will recommend that you see a health visitor or social worker, or will suggest a counsellor to you. Elsewhere, especially outside municipal areas, they might well ask the local nurse to pop in, or even ask the local postman or milkman to keep an eye on you. After all, if you know that someone cares this in itself will ease the pressure.

However limited the time spent, the advantages of talking to any sympathetic uninvolved person are enormous. Often outsiders are able to perceive, much more clearly than those involved, the answer to a problem. Even if you disagree with someone's advice, or even if it is wrong, it can often spark you off to make a right decision, or perversely to come upon a truth neither of you had realized before. You will then be in a position to work out how to go from there.

Accepting that you *are* depressed, lonely and desperate can be the first tentative step on the road to recovery. Pills might seem to be the answer, and might well dull the pain, but often they only prolong the cure.

Your depression will lift, although it is practically impossible for you to believe this at present, when you are in the middle of it. Yet if you do suppress the misery and soldier on, not thinking about how and why you are feeling as you do, you may find the mental anguish emerging as physical ill-health in the form of headaches, sleeplessness, fatigue or irritability.

Take, for example, the case of Jeremy, a young man

whose beloved was killed suddenly: 'Because no one knew of our relationship, when she died I had nobody to talk to about it. My parents would not have understood, and I kept it bottled up. I still felt depressed several years later, although I could not understand why. I went to my doctor, who encouraged me to talk, and he suggested I see a counsellor. I did this, and through their help I eventually came to terms with my grief, talked and cried it out – which I wish I had done at the time.'

AN EXCUSE FOR INACTION
Ill-health can also be used as an easy way to avoid making a move into the outside world again. Instead of fighting off the headache which keeps on recurring, or the cold that just will not go away, you have to stay in. Rather than making a little bit of an effort to start your new life you let your health govern your actions.

You may feel that *only* your partner understood how to look after you when you were ill. You may be reluctant to tell anyone else – friend or colleague – what is wrong, because you will have to explain, and you have not had to do that for a long time, because your partner knew instinctively how you felt.

It is important not to give in to these feelings. You will find that other people can deal with you as well, and might even look after you better than your partner. Give it a go, make the effort and that effort will lead you on to overcome bigger hurdles.

However, on the other side of the coin, it is worth pointing out that for some people, especially women, this may be the first time in years that you have been able to put yourself first without worrying about the rest of the family. In the past you may have felt ill on occasion but brushed the feeling aside because you had a spouse to look after or the house to run. Now you have only yourself to look after, you have time to take more notice of your body and its indications that all is not well. If you have children to look after, it is even more important to consider your health, especially if you have disregarded it before.

A common trap people fall into, which does not only apply to the 'suddenly single', is putting down feelings of ill-health to age. One 50-year-old woman recently told a friend that she often felt ill, with pains in her stomach after eating. She thought it was just because she was getting on and was suffering from indigestion. She eventually went to the doctor to be told that she had a small ulcer. As soon as this was remedied she was as right as rain. Age did not enter into it.

ALCOHOL AND DRUGS

In times of stress it is all too easy to blot out the pain with alcohol or drugs. Neither of them solves the problem, and they will eventually make matters worse.

The abuse of alcohol is probably more widely recognized, but the ease with which drugs can be obtained, either legally through prescription or illegally off the streets, is frightening. At best they can carry you through for a short time, but alcohol and drugs carry the risk of addiction, which can do nothing but destroy your life.

If you feel you are in danger of becoming dependent on either alcohol or drugs do not hesitate to act. See your doctor, or get in touch immediately with one of the relevant organizations (see Chapter 13).

FITNESS

Keeping fit does not mean jogging every morning for ten miles, swimming 40 lengths of a pool or working out in a gym every day. Most people know in their heart of hearts whether they are fit or not. Are you out of breath after walking up a flight of stairs or running for the bus? Have you stopped looking in the mirror because of all those extra bulges? If so, perhaps you should start forgetting to take the car to the shops round the corner, and walk instead.

If you are excessively overweight, do something about losing it. This does not mean crash dieting, just eating less of everything and cutting out obviously fattening things such as cream, sugar and fried food. And if you lead a very sedentary existence, start taking some exercise.

Walking is a cheap and enjoyable way to exercise. It will not help you lose much weight, but it will benefit the body – muscles, heart and lungs – if you do it briskly and regularly. Running could be the next stage, once you have built up a basic level of fitness. You could take up cycling – on your own or with friends – instead of using the car. It will get fresh air into the lungs, tone the muscles and burn off some excess calories. But if you have not been on a bicycle for some time, begin by taking it easy.

Dancing is another obvious answer to the exercise question, because the benefits of what you have achieved in your dance classes can be reaped socially as well as in terms of physical well-being.

Swimming is one of the best forms of exercise. It uses many muscles in the body and is always exhilarating.

If you enjoyed tennis, squash or badminton at school, consider joining a local club. You will not be the only person who is rusty, or learning to play the game, and as well as doing your health a power of good you will be meeting people on a regular basis.

Perhaps you could try a few exercises for ten minutes every morning or evening. There are plenty of books to read that will put you on the right track, but all of them will stress that for the greatest benefit exercises should be done regularly. Try making them part of your routine, like brushing your teeth, so that rather than getting in the way of your day, they are part of it.

Think about any activities you have enjoyed in the past which you may have given up during your marriage or partnership. You will probably find that you still get pleasure from them – and get healthy at the same time. But do check with your doctor first if you intend to embark on any vigorous exercise.

RELAXATION

As well as taking some form of regular exercise, you must also learn how to relax. The body and the mind both need time to unwind. If you are too much on edge even to sit down for half an hour with a book, a newspaper or just a cup of coffee, perhaps you should think about attending some formal course in relaxation (or perhaps a yoga class) to help you cope better with the stress, anxiety or worry you are feeling.

Human beings run on three components: body, mind and emotions. These three should work in harmony, and if one is out of tune it will affect all the others. Real relaxation can benefit all three.

You can relax in many ways, but there are an enormous number of people who do not know how to, or who find it difficult. Reading a book, doing the crossword, lying on your back for ten minutes on the living-room floor, cooking, gardening, dreaming or just soaking in a bath – in fact anything that releases your mind from your worries, even for a short time – are all ways of relaxing.

Susan Balfour, a divorcee, felt she needed to learn how to relax, and went along to some local classes. She found she benefited so much and became so involved that she is now a teacher. 'I run a seven-week course, two hours once a week. I begin each class by helping people understand what is happening to their bodies – why they are getting physical symptoms from mentally related problems – and how to help themselves.

'I demonstrate simple muscle-loosening movements to help relaxation, and then teach the class how to recognize when they are reacting to stress, to be aware when their bodies are tense. The movements can be done during the day, at the bus-stop, sitting at an office desk. For example, some people might not have realized that when talking on the phone they grip the handset so tightly – almost as if they are squeezing it to death. Once they are made aware of what they are doing, they can do something about it.

'I teach both men and women, although men are more reluctant to join, not liking to admit they could possibly benefit from this sort of class.

'I also try to overcome people's blocks. One very common hang-up is that people think they are wasting time by relaxing. They feel that if they are not doing something physically positive, they are being self-indulgent, and could be doing something far more useful with their time. It is difficult for some people to realize, and let themselves feel, what it is like to be relaxed. Once they discover how nice it is to be relaxed, and not to be guilty about it, they enjoy it. If you cannot give time to yourself to replenish your mind and body, how can you be fit to go about your work, or help anybody else?'

BEING ILL
If you are feeling ill and are on your own, or alone with a young child, do see your doctor. Do not put it off. A visit can do no harm, whereas if you try to ignore the symptoms you may find that the following day you are not even in a fit enough state to phone the doctor.

Of course you are aware that doctors get fed up with

hypochondriacs, people who waste their time by imagining that they are ill. But the chances are that if you are afraid of being a hypochondriac, you are unlikely to be one.

If you are feeling low, a few hours in bed can often be better than any amount of medicine. Again, do not be afraid to ask for help. Ring a neighbour or friend (perhaps one who has been asking whether there is anything he or she can do to help you) and ask him/her to pick up your milk and groceries, see to any small domestic problems that are worrying you, pick up your children from school or even heat up some soup for you.

If you have a bad cold you will get over it more quickly by staying in bed all day and sleeping as much as you can than you will by struggling on. You score no points for being a martyr.

If you have young children, ask someone you know well, perhaps the parents of one of their friends, to take them off your hands for a few hours so you can have the rest you need, or maybe have them to stay for a couple of days.

If you have a job, your work will suffer if you are not up to par. There is a lot of difference between malingering and taking time off work to recover from illness.

If you are having a problem getting help, do not send yourself into a frenzy. There are voluntary and local authority organizations that can help. Do not be afraid to ring them. (See Chapter 13.)

EATING PROPERLY

It is easy to fall into bad eating habits when you are on your own. Elaine, a widow of 65, explained her attitude, which is unfortunately all too typical: 'I have never really enjoyed cooking. I can't be bothered just for myself. I only cook when the children come down for the weekend, which is not that often. Otherwise, I live on toast and very little else.' Shortly after making this statement Elaine was diagnosed as suffering from malnutrition, and was ordered by her doctor to eat a balanced diet.

Men are often very careless about what they eat. Barry, aged 33 and divorced, recalled his situation: 'I must admit, to my shame, I had never learnt to cook. So when I found myself on my own I survived on tins and take-aways. When I hit a bad patch, my doctor was so frustrated with me that he actually bought me a book on cooking for one.

And I found having a balanced diet has made a lot of difference to how I feel. Funnily enough, now I find cooking – having come back from a fraught day at the office – very relaxing and soothing. And I am beginning to get quite adventurous.'

Even people with children are at risk. They feed their children properly, but they make do with leftovers for themselves, perhaps filling up with a packet of crisps or a jam sandwich.

To keep in good health you must eat correctly. Just as your car needs the right fuel to run properly, so do you. You would not dream of putting oil, water or alcohol in your petrol tank. So how can you expect to 'run' efficiently if you have not provided yourself with the right fuel?

Try to eat a balanced diet, which means a regular supply of fresh vegetables, fruit, meat, fish and dairy products. Include plenty of fibre (found in fruit, vegetables, wholemeal bread, wholemeal pasta and brown rice, and muesli-type breakfast cereals), and cut out sugar as much as you can. This may seem obvious to many people, but it is all too easy to live on bread and cheese, or eggs, and think you are eating enough to be healthy. Check with your doctor if you think you are not eating the right things.

Vegetarians can live well without meat, but may do well to take extra vitamins to supplement any they may be missing in their diet.

By learning to relax, talking to people, not hiding or suppressing your grief, working through your problems and not letting pride or bravado hinder your progress, you will regain your peace of mind. And by eating sensibly and staying physically active, you will stay fit and healthy and well able to withstand the emotional trauma you are going through.

CHAPTER 6

Sex and sexuality

'Sex' means different things to different people. It can mean sexuality. It can mean sexual intercourse. It can mean the touching, kissing, and cuddling that is part of making love, or the physical presence of someone beside you in bed. It can also mean pure animal lust.

Asked what they felt about sex since they had been left on their own, people's answers varied from 'I miss my loving wife' to 'More than sex I miss someone to touch and hold'; 'Having split up from my husband, I couldn't face the thought of never having sex with him again and when I went out with other men I felt as if I was committing adultery'; 'I've totally lost any interest in sex'; 'Great. I had a lot of wasted time to catch up on'; 'I can take it or leave it. It's the person I care about'; and 'I was amazed to find it could be better'.

There is no 'norm' for how people feel about sex. If you feel you never want to think about it again, that is fine, but it is unlikely that you will feel like that for ever; if you decide you are ready for new relationships, then go ahead.

When you become single you have to work out for yourself what you want in terms of a sex life, putting aside what you thought you wanted, or what you think people will expect you to want. It is your decision and whatever you decide is right for you is the correct answer. You may have lost confidence in your sexuality, your ability to be attractive and to be loved by another person, possibly because your previous partner denigrated and rejected you, and made you feel unloved. But you can regain your self-confidence and self-respect.

There is no right or wrong in what you do. Whether you choose to live a celibate life for a few months, or even years; whether sex is something for which you are prepared to wait until you re-marry; whether you want occasional sexual relationships; whether you want to experience sex with many people, the important factor is to work out what will make you happy – not forgetting the person or people with whom you might involve yourself. If you are just using others to prove to yourself that you are still sexually attractive, think about the effect you might be having on them. You have been hurt yourself. Surely you do not want to do the same to another human being?

LEARNING FROM THE PAST

Look back over your previous sexual relationships and feelings about sex; reassess what sex meant to you and your partner: having the time to think on your own, particularly now that there is no one to influence you, means you can be true to yourself. Were you in your previous sexual relationship? Hundreds of people, through fear and ignorance rather than dishonesty, cheat and lie in their sexual relationships, especially in feigning a greater enjoyment of it than they have ever in fact felt.

When you look back, were you really happy with your sex life, or was it just something which had to be done? At the time you might have felt happy with it, but was this because it was easy, because it made your partner happy or because the other things you got out of the relationship made sex less important to you?

The idea of a 'good sex life' is largely an invention of the media, which has established a yardstick by which we feel obliged to measure our own relationships. It suggests a high level of adventurous sexual activity, and we are intimidated into believing that if we have a 'good sex life' we will have a good relationship; if we have a 'bad sex life' our whole relationship is doomed.

Sex *is* important, but it is only one facet of a relationship, and is perhaps far less important than the media would have us believe. There are no rules as to what is good or bad in sex. The only important thing is that you and your partner should enjoy it and be happy and feel close to one another. Sex can be very spiritual, yet what is spiritually uplifting and bonding for one couple might seem disgusting to another. But there can be nothing perverted in sex as long as both partners enjoy it.

Sex is more than just a way of expressing yourself; it is part of being with somebody. Achieving fulfilment from sex does not mean making love every night, having orgasms or working your way through the *Kama Sutra*. True fulfilment can only come through understanding yourself, your own needs and hang-ups and those of your partner.

Sex can often become a means of establishing supremacy in a relationship, putting somebody down, proving you are better. Did this sort of competitiveness ever enter into your former relationship?

Looking back, how many times did you want to tell your partner what you felt about your sexual relationship, but did not dare because you were frightened either of revealing your true feelings or of his or her reactions? Unless you can be honest with your partner you cannot hope for a satisfactory relationship.

But to be honest with someone, you have to be honest with yourself, and often dishonesty in a relationship stems from dishonesty in sex. It is not easy to overcome childhood or adolescent hang-ups, perhaps instilled into you by friends, parents or bad experiences at an early age.

Sex is about giving and receiving, and if you cannot give, you are unlikely to receive or be able to enjoy receiving. In terms of working out one's sexual life giving is very important. Giving in is not the same. Whereas on other parts of your relationship you can, on the surface, float along, with sex it is much more difficult and as a result much more frightening, for both men and women.

Many people who have married for a second time find they have a more fulfilling and successful sex life than they did in their first one. The woman has thought more about what she wants, is likely to be more honest in letting her partner know how she feels and consequently gets more satisfaction; and the man, having worried about what he might have been doing wrong when his first marriage broke up, takes a greater interest in his new partner's desires and is more eager to please.

Your sexual boundaries are set very soon after marrying. Most people find it difficult, after a long relationship, to adapt to a new one, but if you use the knowledge you bring to it to build a better one, you will reap the benefits.

REACTIONS TO LOSING A PARTNER

Dorothy, 45, had been widowed. She felt life had treated her harshly and could not face the thought of a new partnership: 'My husband died suddenly two years ago. It was so unexpected, I feel cheated. We had so much more to experience together, so many things to do. I also feel cheated in sex. I am not interested in starting another relationship, after 24 happy, happy years. That doesn't mean I have lost my sex drive, but even more than sex I miss holding hands and cuddling.'

Timothy, 37, divorced after fifteen years of marriage, took a rational look back at what had happened: 'The first ten years were blissfully happy, then things started going wrong. We had two children, and for their sake we tried to make the marriage work. Eventually I realized it would be better, rather than worse, for them if we parted. I missed the physical side of our relationship, but I also missed the pleasure of being able to touch someone – during a conversation, just giving her a hug because I wanted to, having a cuddle in the afternoon or over breakfast.'

Frances, 26, divorced after five years of marriage, needed to prove to herself that she could still be wanted and loved: 'I felt very frustrated and desperate to have a relationship with anyone who showed desire, because I needed to feel attractive to men. After the bad scene with my husband – he had had an affair, and I couldn't stand that – I felt I must be unattractive to him and to anyone else. I thought no one would fancy me again. So I found it very comforting to know I could still be wanted, and was thrilled to re-discover my own libido. Now my confidence has returned, so has my self-respect. I can enjoy life again.'

John, 40, described the freedom he suddenly felt after an unhappy marriage which ended suddenly after ten years: 'Although I felt great inadequacy that I had not been able to repair the relationship, I was also glad it was over. When we broke up, I felt like a person presented with an *à la carte* menu the day of ending a diet. I had felt so trapped in my marriage that when I was single again I felt free.'

Sarah, 35, who left her husband after fourteen years, explained how difficult she found it to adjust to someone else's routine: 'I missed sex a lot, the physical release and the tenderness and touching involved. It took a while to re-gain my self-respect and when I eventually entered onto another sexual relationship I found it difficult to accept somebody else's attitudes, that he had his own life to lead, his feelings about cuddling and kissing. It was hard to adjust to someone else who had his own schedules. My ex-husband used to make me a cup of tea first thing in the morning; my lover expected *me* to do it! My ex used to leave the house early, before I got up. Suddenly I found myself being the first one to get dressed. All these things are not important, but having been used to a way of life it is very strange starting all over again. And because I had been on my own for a year before I met David, I had also begun to enjoy being my own boss.'

The following three interviewees showed completely different attitudes to sex. The first was not worried about the lack of sex life, the second felt she had been cheated, and the third worried that he would never have such a good physical relationship again.

Geraldine, 32, had been married for nine years: 'My marriage had been going wrong for some time. I wasn't interested in sex with my husband for some time before the break-up. Then I was numb for a long time after he left. Later I wanted a sexual relationship, but felt at first it was a bit like seeing if I could still ride a bike after not doing so for so long.'

'We had just started getting our sex life really together,' explained Belinda, 25, who had been widowed suddenly. 'We were both so naive when we married, and had been learning together how great it can be. Now I've got to start all over with someone else. I suppose I know more than I did before we married, but I wanted it to be good with him.'

Jim, 32, had been divorced. For his marriage a good sex life had not been enough: 'Our sex life was great. But it didn't keep the marriage going. One of the things I worry about is that it was so good: will I ever be able to find the same thing again?'

Colin, 39, had been married for six years. He had not lost his libido, but he did feel he wanted to keep away from making serious commitments: 'I left suddenly, after a year of great unhappiness. I knew my wife had a lover and although I still loved her, I got to the stage where I just couldn't take any more. I never went off sex, and being on my own I wanted to have relationships with women that weren't going to tie me down, whom I wouldn't have to get involved with. Although these relationships were very short-lived they gave me back the confidence that I had lost. This was because I was made to feel there was hope left that I might eventually find another partner.'

NEW RELATIONSHIPS

For many people suffering from loneliness or grief after losing a partner, there is a strong urge to find a new one – anyone – as soon as possible: it is described as 'love on the rebound'. Though this may just be a way of seeking solace, many end up getting hurt by the experience – or being hurtful to the person they have 'used'. Be aware of your vulnerability, but, on the other hand, do not let suspicion get in the way. If a new relationship seems to be going well and you are happy about this, give it a chance, but take it slowly. Avoid rushing into major commitments: they may seem to be a quick solution to ending loneliness, but you could be making a mistake that will take far longer to undo than to make.

A doctor told me a sad story of a male friend of his who was engaged to be married, but was killed in a car accident a month before the wedding. After his fiancée had recovered from the shock, she started going out with his brother and very soon they got married. A year later she realized she had married on the rebound, and she (and her new husband) had to go through the unhappiness of parting and starting again.

After separation or divorce, you go through a process of learning from your last relationship. By working through your emotions and looking back, or by accepting and understanding the problems that beset you in your previous relationship, you can make yourself a stronger, more complete person. You will find this experience can help you to cope better with a new partnership. And you should not be frightened of starting another relationship. If you have managed to overcome great misery and loneliness, you have nothing more to fear.

When you start a new relationship, take it gradually. Try not to build your hopes too high. And if the relationship is not working, get out of it. It is sometimes hard to believe it when you have just split up with or lost somebody, but there are hundreds of people out there who could be right for you. Just make sure you choose the right one.

As Jonathan said, after leaving his wife of three years, 'It is better to be alone than with the wrong person.'

There is another danger in rushing into a new sexual relationship with the first willing stranger to come along: sexual disease. If after sexual intercourse with a new partner you notice a discharge, or feel sore or itchy, go straight to your doctor or to a VD clinic. It is far better to endure a little embarrassment than risk having or carrying an infection. If a disease is confirmed you will be asked to reveal the name and address of your partner, and he or she in turn will be asked to give the names and addresses of previous sexual partners. You may not want to do this, but such information is essential if the spread of disease is to be checked; it will be treated in the strictest confidence.

IMPOTENCE AND RETURN OF SEXUAL FEELINGS

After a divorce, or the death of a wife, it is not uncommon for men to become impotent. This may be due to a lack of confidence, respect for the wife's memory or, if the marriage broke up, a feeling of failure and rejection. Impotence is a normal reaction to emotional upsets, but it is usually a temporary problem.

If you abstain from sexual intercourse for a while, the chances are that the problem will sort itself out. It is often just a question of relaxation and confidence, and of being frank with your new partner. Stress – worrying about money, not seeing your children, problems at work – commonly affects people's sexual performance. As those pressures ease, your enjoyment of sex will probably return. Obviously, if the impotence persists, or is worrying you unduly, you should see your doctor, or a trained sex therapist. Talking the problem out is often the first step to solving it.

After a break-up, but more especially if they have been widowed, many women do not want to think about or even consider having sex. They think they will never have sexual feelings again, and are not bothered by the idea of being celibate and staying faithful forever to the partner they have lost. Sometimes this is the case, and they can be perfectly happy in this state. But more often than not sexual feelings do return – anything from a month to years afterwards. When they do, and you find yourself unexpectedly fancying another man, do not feel guilty – you are not being cruel or unfaithful to the husband you once loved, or to his memory. It is natural for sexual feelings to surface again.

If you are confused by your sexual feelings, worried, or feeling guilty and have no close friend to whom you can talk, do go to your doctor, or a counsellor.

CHAPTER 7

Work

Whatever the circumstances that made you single, it is likely that the question of money, and therefore, perhaps, of employment, may be one of the first matters of which you will have to take stock.

For many people, the economic necessity of having to keep up their jobs is one of the things which has kept them going.

James, 37, who separated from his wife after five years, certainly found this was the case: 'I was running my own business, and after the split I threw myself into making it work. If I hadn't had that, I would have had nothing. There were problems with seeing the children, and emotionally I was very low. Some nights I even slept at the office, because I couldn't stand returning to my cheap digs. For the first time in my life, the difficulties at work seemed a blessing.'

Sheila, a widow of 47, said: 'If I had not had to go into work, to concentrate on what I was doing and have some reason to get up in the morning, I think I would have lost my sanity. I found it incredibly difficult concentrating at work, but I made myself do it – probably going over things three times, rather than once, to check myself. Having to make an effort every day stopped me wallowing in despair and self-pity. So many mornings I thought, "I'll turn over and go back to sleep", but then I remembered the people who were relying on me at the office, and I couldn't let them down.'

At times you may feel unable to carry on working. You lack application, you break down in tears and cannot do what you previously took in your stride. Lacking concentration is very common if you are suffering from loss or grief, and it will pass in time. In most cases an understanding boss will allow you time off, but in the long run the discipline of having to get up to go to work, put your mind to something other than your emotional problems and be among other people can be vital.

Gloria, a young widow who found she was hopeless at home – cutting her fingers on the bread knife, dropping things, forgetting to turn taps off – said: 'Although it was impossible to function at home, at work I found my mind was clear. I was able to keep my job going; I didn't make mistakes. But at home I just went to pieces. I couldn't do anything properly.'

Susan, 52, found that work provided a helpful pattern to the day: 'I went back to work two weeks after my husband's death. Returning to work quickly did help. It made me dress up, do my hair, face up to things, get into a routine as quickly as possible. By keeping my life going, I found it helped to dull the dreadful ache.'

Jane, widowed in her late forties, experienced her greatest problems at the times she was not working: 'My work gave me the routine I needed when I couldn't bear to think about the future. But I hated coming back to an empty house in the evening. I started making arrangements to meet people after work, going out to the theatre, having a meal out. Then I realized I was overspending. So I made myself go home as I did before, but instead of doing what I used to do – sitting down on the sofa, pouring a drink – I altered my habits. I learnt yoga, and spent the first half an hour doing that. Somehow that made the emptiness of the house less overpowering.'

Many people feel they have to keep as busy as they can, throwing themselves into their jobs, taking on extra work, doing a course in the evenings and at weekends. This is fine as long as you are not denying yourself your grief. Being busy is a good thing, but being too busy is not. It is easy to tire yourself out and then find you have no time or energy for anything you really want to do. And if you are trying to get over the emotional trauma of break-up or the loss of a spouse, you need to look after yourself: relaxation plays a part in the healing process (see Chapter 5) and suffering from exhaustion is not the way to recovery.

PART-TIME WORK
If you have not worked before, but are feeling that enough time has passed for you to feel like doing something, you could try a part-time job.

You might not have a clue what you can do, or want to do. A good starting point is to jot down on a piece of paper all the things you enjoy doing, and are good at – anything from cooking to making toys, driving cars, looking after children, being good with figures, or even ironing shirts. Then try to put those talents to use. For example, if you like flowers, ask local florists whether they need an extra hand, perhaps at weekends when they are short-staffed, which is probably when *you* feel most alone.

You might be very happy doing a job that someone else would find boring, such as gardening or mending clothes (see pages 48–9). Put an advertisement in your local paper or shop window and see what sort of response you get.

If you are receiving supplementary benefit, family income supplement or a pension, work out, or ask the local social security office to work out for you, how much you can earn without affecting your benefits. (See also Chapter 14.)

Working in a school
If you have children, a job in a school could be ideal for you. Your holidays would coincide with theirs, and the job need not have anything to do with teaching; schools also need bursars, secretaries, cleaners, dinner supervisors and so on. Apply to the local education authority to see what is available.

Running a playgroup
If you have young children, perhaps you might consider starting a playgroup for under-fives. There is always a shortage of them, and as well as not having to leave your own children you will be helping other parents. Other mothers are bound to be interested, and some will want to help. You could contact your local authority to see what other groups exist in your area; alternatively, a social worker or health visitor might be able to advise you.

Learning a new skill
There are many courses open to mature students through which you could learn a new skill or improve on the ones you have. As well as possibly increasing your earning power and job-satisfaction, taking a course – especially evening classes – could well stave off loneliness at the times

when you are most aware of it. If you have young children whom you cannot leave, you could try a correspondence course. The Department of Education and Science and your local authority will have details. (See Chapter 13.)

Voluntary work
If you do not need to work for money, you may be more interested in voluntary work. You will find that there are many organizations, associations and local authorities who would be delighted to have your help. The Citizens' Advice Bureau and your local library can provide information about voluntary work in your area. (See also Bibliography.)

EARNING MONEY AT HOME
If you have retained the family home, it is possible that it is too big for you. One way of supplementing your income is let some rooms, but you will, of course, have to pay tax on the extra income if it takes you above your personal allowances.

You could take a lodger, maybe a student who just needs a room in term-time. If you have children away at college or university this could work very well; moreover, you would not be alone in the house at night, and you would have someone else to talk to and think about. On the other hand, if it did not work out, you would not have to put up with the situation for very long.

You could help someone who is looking for a house or waiting to move into your area and only needs somewhere to live temporarily. Alternatively, you might wish to have a tenant on a lease basis. But before you take anybody into your home, consult a solicitor about the legal aspects of tenancy. (See Chapter 11.)

You might consider offering bed and breakfast. It would involve extra washing, cleaning and providing a good breakfast in the morning, but you may prefer very short-term guests to the risk of taking on a lodger with whom you might not see eye to eye.

MAKING HOBBIES PAY
Why not make some money out of your hobby? For example, if you like cooking, you might be able to sell cakes or pâtés to local retailers, or fully-assembled dishes to a restaurant or café. You could also investigate vacancies for

cooks. If you can make clothes or knit, you could become an outworker for a manufacturing company or even supply a local boutique direct. If you love tinkering with cars, perhaps you could work on somebody else's and earn a few extra pounds.

You can always find something useful or money-making to do if you put a little thought and effort into it, but do beware of the very low rates of pay in some cottage industries. Exploitation is rife, for example, among outworkers in the garment business.

Your hobby could be channelled into helping a charity. This is what Janice, a middle-aged widow, discovered; she explained: 'I have great fun collecting woollens from all over and from all sorts of different people. I unwind them and put the wool into skeins. I wash this, dry it, roll it back into balls and take it to my sister who makes gloves. We sell these and the money goes to St Mary's Hospice. I also do a little voluntary work at the Queen Elizabeth Hospital, and make Christmas decorations and gift tags which I sell, and I give the money to the hospice.'

CHANGING JOBS
Like moving house, it is unwise to make a decision about leaving your job very soon after divorce or bereavement. You may feel strongly that you must change your whole way of life in order to forget the past, and you may be right in deciding to change your job, but it is a matter for careful consideration rather than immediate action. If you were to make the wrong decision you could well find yourself unhappy in your new job and wishing you were back at your old work-place where you had friends.

However, if you are currently in a job where you are unhappy, it would be better to leave and try to find somewhere to work where you will be happy as part of your general plan for getting to grips with a new life. Some people do not enjoy their jobs and do not particularly get on with their workmates, but they put up with the situation because it brings in money and is counterbalanced by the happiness they get from their home life. You are presumably not in such a position.

When you have given yourself a few months to recover and find out what you do want, you may well decide that starting again in a new area is the right thing to do.

Depending on the sort of job you are looking for, shop windows can be as good a place to look as employment agencies and labour exchanges; look at the job advertisements in local and national newspapers and specialist national magazines; talk to as many people you can about job opportunities and keep your options open. If you hide the fact that you are looking for a job from friends and acquaintances you may narrow your chances of finding one.

Bear in mind that job-hunting, especially in a difficult economic climate, needs energy, determination and resilience. Can you withstand the possibility of repeated rejections if you have yourself been recently rejected by your partner? Do you feel good enough about yourself to project a positive, cheerful attitude at a job interview? No employer wants to take on a miserable, self-obsessed employee.

However if you have been left suddenly on your own you will find it hard enough going through this difficult time without the added burden of being unhappy at work. It may be better to leave that job and try to find something you will enjoy, even if it pays less well.

And maybe the energy taken up job-hunting will help you get over the pain and emptiness you feel.

CHAPTER 8

Children

One in eight families in Britain is a one-parent family. Of these, 84.4 per cent are headed by women, 12.6 per cent by men, and that means 1,000,000 divorced, single and widowed parents caring for 1,500,000 children. They are therefore very much part of the fabric of society, but unfortunately the state is still centred economically, legally and socially on families of two adults and 2.2 children.

It is very important to explain to your children, if they are old enough to understand, that you are separating, divorcing, or that their father or mother has died. If the marriage is breaking up, you must try hard not to denigrate or put down your partner in front of the children. However much you may hate your partner, he or she is still the child's parent. The courts can dissolve marriages, but they cannot dissolve parenthood.

If you have been bereaved, you will find it hard to explain to your child what has happened, especially when you are feeling at your lowest ebb, but this is not a task you can delegate. If the child is to understand, and to be able to grieve, you must make the effort.

Children are not stupid. If there is separation in the air you can be assured they will have sensed something is going on. Rather than keeping children in the dark – often mistakenly thought by adults to be 'protecting' them – tell them what is going to happen. If a child knows something 'bad' is happening, but nothing is explained, it may cause a worse trauma. The child might feel guilty and blame himself; he might think he is going to lose both parents, he might feel anger, resentment or rejection, and he will almost certainly be confused.

How you tell or explain to your children that your marriage is coming to an end will depend on the age and character of each individual. There is no right or wrong way of approaching the subject, but as you know your children better than anyone else you should be able to find a way of telling them and at the same time reassuring them of your love, and your partner's love, for them. If your children do seem to be suffering, and you are not sure how best to help them, conciliation and counselling associations can help. (See Chapter 13.)

If your children ask questions, try to answer them as clearly and confidently as you can. They will not need long, detailed accounts, just reassurance. By being honest and keeping them informed throughout, they will be able to deal with it in their own way with your help.

If your children are young and are missing the other parent very much, it can sometimes help to get them a pet. This may sound frivolous, but it can work. Most children love animals, and having one of their own to care for and love will divert them from the family crisis. You will probably have to do some of the cleaning and feeding, but the inconvenience could prove well worth while.

This approach certainly worked with Anthony, whose father died when he was six. For several months after his father's death, he suffered violent stomach-aches. He went into hospital for tests and at first it was thought he had appendicitis. Then ulcers were suspected. Eventually the doctor decided there was nothing wrong with him at all. He suggested that Anthony's mother should buy him a pony; when she did, the symptoms soon disappeared.

Of course, the pet you buy for your children does not have to be a horse, or even a dog or cat. If you have room, a rabbit might be a good idea. Otherwise, a white mouse or hamster can be just as rewarding: these need only a small cage to live in and are relatively cheap to feed. Even a goldfish or a budgerigar could provide the answer.

If your partner has died, explain to your children what has happened. Usually, even children as young as four years old can understand. Knowing the truth, in whatever way they perceive it, will help them come through it – as you will – and will save you the agony of answering repeated enquiries about the return of the absent partner.

If dealt with sensitively, the children's experience of loss will hold them in good stead in future years; for they will have learnt, albeit at an early age, that loss and grief can be overcome and that it is not the end of the world when someone close to them goes away.

It is important to talk to your children about death, and to let them cry. Just as you must allow yourself to grieve, so must your children feel free to do so. Try not to stop them sobbing their hearts out in their pillow at night. Instead go and comfort them and if you feel like it cry with them. It will do you both good and it will let your child see that crying is not something of which to be ashamed. If they see their mother or father holding their emotions back, or appearing not to grieve, they may feel guilty about showing their own grief openly.

GOING TO THE FUNERAL
Your decision as to whether your child should attend the funeral depends entirely on the child's personality and temperament. Some, especially those with the benefit of a religious upbringing, could find it comforting to see a gathering of people who loved the deceased parent pay their last respects and hear the clergyman's words of assurance and comfort; such children might indeed feel hurt and left out if they are not allowed to attend. Other children, especially younger ones, might be frightened by it and even with sensitive preparation on the part of the remaining parent could be severely traumatized by events at the crematorium or the graveside. If a child does not want to go to the funeral, you should not force him to go.

CHILDREN'S QUESTIONS
One of the greatest difficulties in dealing with children after a death is their perpetual questioning. 'Where is Daddy?' or 'When is Mummy coming back?' can be awkward and upsetting enquiries to cope with when you are in a state of shock yourself. But it is important to make the effort to try to explain the situation the best you can.

A friend whose mother died recently had a couple of children in their early teens, both girls. When the grandmother died he refrained from telling his children immediately. When they were told, and found out that their granny had in fact died some days before, they were angry and felt they had been left out on purpose.

SOLACE FROM CHILDREN
Children who are old enough to understand can be a great strength to parents, and by providing comfort they can feel

better in themselves, because they know they are able to help and do something constructive.

Martha found that the death of her husband brought her even closer to her 17-year-old son: 'Tom has been a great comfort to me. He became a man overnight. He has become very protective towards me, and although he is away at college he phones me every two or three days.'

For others, just having the children around was the greatest comfort they could have.

THE ABSENT PARENT

If one parent has left the family home, the first thing to do is to explain the situation to your children. You need to stress, over and over again if necessary, that although Mummy or Daddy has left home and that you do not love each other any more, you both still love your children deeply. It is important for children not to feel rejected by either parent.

Gill, whose husband left her suddenly without warning and went abroad, described her predicament: 'I didn't know what to tell my children, who were 10 and 8 at the time, because I didn't know what was happening myself. I told them as much as I knew and did my best to reassure them that their daddy still loved them, although as he didn't write to them or phone them this was pretty difficult. Three years later I discovered where he was and we made contact again. He now writes to them and sends them presents.'

'USING' YOUR CHILDREN

It is difficult not to involve your children when there is bitterness and anger in the separation or divorce. There is a great temptation to use them as weapons against your spouse, ask them to 'spy' for you and let yourself 'bad-mouth' your partner when you should be keeping those feelings to yourself. Sound off about him or her to friends, by all means, but not to your children. The person you are putting down is your child's parent, whom your child loves. They have a right to see each other and to continue their parent/child relationship.

Try not to pressurize your children or divide their loyalties. It will not do you any good. If you have used your children against your ex-partner, when they grow up and realize what you have done they could turn against you.

It is also important not to promise your children what is not possible. If a parent has left and is not going to see the children again, do not pretend that he or she will. Your children will only have their hopes raised to see them dashed when the promises fall apart.

YOUR 'EX' AND YOUR CHILDREN
Many divorcees who have custody of children feel guilty about depriving their partners of their children. If you are considering divorce, this can quite often stop you from taking the final step.

Susan, who had been married for fourteen years, had two children of eight and four: 'It was very hard seeing my ex-husband hugging the children in desperation after an outing. We both knew that basically *I* had the children. Although he had unlimited access, it was not the same.'

Of course this is not always the case: Jean, 30, who left her husband when her daughter was six, has no regrets that her daughter has not seen her father since.

'My husband was violent,' she explained. 'Funnily enough I didn't mind him hitting me. I got used to it. It was when he hit Sara that I knew I had to leave immediately, whatever the consequences. I know Sara feels perfectly secure with me. . . It was a relief to us both when we left, and it has brought us closer together.'

It is all too easy to feel jealous if your children become fond of the 'new parent'. But you should be glad that they are happy with the new situation.

It is not fair on children to try to try to find out through them about your ex, or your ex's new partner, if there is one, or to ask them to take sides. Do not ask your children to carry messages or act as go-betweens, and do not try to use them to get your partner back.

Liza, whose husband had left her for another woman, tried to do this, with disastrous results: 'In extreme desperation I thought the only way to make him come back was through making my child ill. I gave her a whole lot of sleeping pills, phoned my husband and told him what I had done. He phoned the ambulance and she was rushed to hospital, and, thank God, she recovered completely.

'Of course, he didn't come back. I not only lost his respect, as well as any love there was left between us. I lost my daughter, who was taken into care.'

If there is acrimony between you and your ex, the child may well play you off against the 'new parent'. This will hurt you, but you will only have yourself to blame.

Children can of course become jealous of the absent parent's new life even if there is no newly-acquired partner.

Dorothy's son of six visited his father quite happily for several months until he saw him looking after the children of the people with whom he was staying. This caused problems, as Dorothy explained: 'My son couldn't bare the thought of his father being involved with other children. David found out he took them to school every morning, as he had previously taken him, and he thought he was no longer important to or loved by his father. So he stopped wanting to see him. Only by both of us talking about it, explaining and giving him masses of love has David come round.'

It is also as well to remember that in some family situations one parent may be away for such long periods of time that it is almost as if the child were part of a one-parent family. In such cases, when the marriage breaks up the child does not have to cope with an abrupt change of lifestyle. In fact, the child can often benefit, because when the other parent visits he or she will probably make a bigger effort to show affection to the child than was previously the case.

Another point to bear in mind, if you are trying to work out whether to make a break or not, is that love and security from one parent is far better for any child than living with two warring ones.

EXPLAINING YOUR EX'S NEW LIFE

When your ex-partner starts going out with someone else, you must be very careful not to show the jealousy, anger or bitterness you may feel to your children.

If you are feeling such emotions you must try your hardest to overcome them, because they could have a destructive effect on you, your ex and your children.

If, for instance, the children are upset because they are no longer the centre of attention when they visit your ex, they will need your help to come to terms with their father's or mother's new relationship. It would be all too easy for you to make things worse, rather than better, but you must resist the urge to turn them against your former partner.

Life goes on, for all concerned. Try not to grudge others a chance of happiness.

INTRODUCING A NEW PARTNER
If someone comes into your life, and especially if he or she is likely to become a permanent fixture, introduce your children to this person gradually, allowing them to get to know each other. Be very careful not to make your children feel unwanted, out of place or less important in your eyes. If your new partner is unsure about meeting your children, do not push it. He or she can always meet them later on when you are both more settled.

Do not play your new partner off against the children's other parent. That will only put pressure on them to take sides, make judgements when they do not want to or cannot do so, and make the whole situation very hard for them to handle. If your new partner tries to put pressure on you or the children in respect of the other parent, put a stop to it.

DISCIPLINE
Another problem which single parents can find difficult to cope with, especially mothers, is having to discipline the children on their own. Unpleasant tasks such as this are easier for two parents to handle than one.

Aileen, who has two small girls, felt very strongly about this: 'As the children get older, I miss another voice of command. I find no problem with their seeing their father, as the situation is quite accepted where I live. So many other friends have similar lifestyles. But I do find it difficult keeping them under control. I suppose I was so used to saying, "Daddy wouldn't like it".'

John, who was left with a girl of five and a boy of nine, faced the same predicament: 'I was abroad with my work when the children were very young, so I really didn't know them that well. When my wife died suddenly I found it extremely hard not to spoil the children, to make up for the loss of their mother. I realized I didn't know how far to let them go, how much to tell them off. I had left that all up to my wife.'

This situation has to be tackled as soon as possible. Children will soon test you to see how far they can go, and once you let them get their own way you will find it difficult to regain control. Allowing your children complete freedom does neither them nor you any good. They will find it much easier to live within a framework and you must work out what rules you want to play by and stick to them. It will make your life easier too. Once the rules are established, try to stick to them, however tired or weak you may be feeling, and regardless of how much your children fight against them.

Do not worry that you will lose their affection. As long as you reassure your children after you have reprimanded them that you still love them and are only telling them off for their own good, they will respect you and they will not love you any less. Be prepared for them to say hurtful things: children are very good at knowing your weak points. So do not react to goading. They may sulk for a while, or seem resentful, but soon something else will take their attention.

THE NON-CUSTODIAL PARENT

In most divorces one parent is given custody of the children and the other is granted access to see them. It is still quite rare for joint custody to be granted, in which one parent has 'care and control', looking after the day-to-day needs of the children, and both parents take responsibility for the major decisions regarding their children's lives, such as education, religion and so on.

The situation is often very difficult for the non-custodial parent because he or she is to a great extent left out of the child's life. Some people find it so hard to deal with that they end up not making the effort to see their children and losing touch; they risk being branded as non-caring and selfish.

More often than not running away is the only way such individuals can cope with their sense of hurt and failure. It cannot be stressed too strongly that both partners in a separation must put aside their own feelings for the sake of the children.

It is vitally important to make access arrangements as simple and as non-disruptive as possible. However hard it may be you must not let your personal disagreement or ego cloud your actions or judgement. If you are having problems sorting out the access arrangements a third party can often help. There are several organizations you can turn to for advice. (See Chapter 13.) Once the access arrangements have been decided upon, do keep to them. To a child, being kept waiting for five minutes seems like hours and the disappointment of cancelled visits can take weeks to get over. Keep to a routine if at all possible; it will give your children the reassurance of stability.

Your child's own needs should be your first consideration. Consider the timing of visits: perhaps having the children on Saturday, because that suits you best, means that they cannot see their friends; or bringing them home at 6.00 pm may mean that some special event or favourite television programme is missed which started at 5.00 pm.

Do not ask the children to decide on the timing of visits, but do listen to their viewpoint. Some parents never consider their children's views seriously, while others ask their children to make important decisions when they are not able to fully understand all the ramifications. Neither action is fair or sensible. However, if you ask your child his opinion, and listen to him – not just to what he says, but how he says it – you are less likely to cause him distress, or to trigger off unreasonable behaviour.

Visits can be traumatic for everyone. The parents must show a united front to their children. Sniping at your ex-partner might make you feel better, but it can damage your children more than you might realize. You must make it as easy as possible for them to come to terms with the new arrangements.

Tony, a divorced father, discovered that his daughter was frightened that her outings with him could endanger her life with her mother: 'I could never understand why Melissa was so awkward with me when I took her out, until one day she blurted out that she thought that when I took her back home Mummy wouldn't be there.'

This is quite a common fear, and particularly at the beginning it is a good idea to see your children in a familiar environment – perhaps at home (the custodial parent can always go out for the day), or maybe at a grandparent's or close friend's home.

If you are a non-custodial parent, finding out how your child is getting on at school can be a problem. With some exceptions, teachers tend to be sympathetic and helpful to the child and the parent with whom he lives, but very often they are less understanding towards the non-custodial parent.

If you are having this problem and your former partner is not being helpful, make an appointment with the headmaster or headmistress, or the child's teacher, so that you can talk things over. In a separation or divorce order you can include being given school reports and information about school activities among your requirements.

Obviously schools do not want to become involved in matrimonial disputes, so if you want to attend school functions, make sure you have worked out who is going to attend, and stick to it. No one wants fraught scenes at the school, least of all your child, who will only be upset and embarrassed.

It is very important for both partners to work out rationally the future of the children. You are both involved with them, if not with each other, and your priority should be to set them up securely and happily for the rest of their lives.

Alan and his partner found this impossible to achieve without a third-party referee. As he explained: 'When we separated there was so much bitterness and animosity that we could hardly speak to each other. Thank God we both realized it would be unbelievably stupid and unforgivable to ruin our children's lives because of our fight. A friend suggested we saw their headmistress, and with her acting as a referee we sorted out what we wanted for our children. I'm sure the head didn't enjoy it but it was so worth while, and the children seem happy. Funnily enough, although the bad feeling between us is still there at least we can communicate sensibly on one level.'

They might have been bad partners, but through divorce they have become better parents.

MONEY PROBLEMS

If you do not have children, the obvious answer is to go out and find a job, if you do not already have one. Working, in whatever capacity, will do a lot for your general morale, and will get you out of the house, as well as increasing your income.

People with children are likely to have more difficult financial problems to solve and the added limitation of having to be at home at certain times for the children. Moreover, while one can scrimp and save for oneself, as an adult, it is not so easy to do this where children are concerned.

First and foremost, then, make sure you are claiming all the benefits to which you are entitled. It is invariably the worse-off who fail to claim the benefits due to them. If you are not sure what your position is, go to your local social security office or an organization which can help (see Chapter 13) and ask advice. Chapter 12 contains a list of the benefits available.

Do not be frightened or embarrassed to speak to your bank manager. He or she is there to help you understand and manage your money and can suggest ways of saving, paying the bills, and generally organizing your money to suit your particular circumstances in the easiest possible way.

LOOKING AFTER CHILDREN

Looking after children on your own is more tiring and more time-consuming than having the help of another pair of hands – even if that extra help may only have been sporadic.

Despite the demands children make on your energy and time, you should try to go out occasionally. Apart from needing to relax, you will benefit from a few hours of adult company. If you need but cannot afford a babysitter, try getting in touch with other mothers to work out a rota for looking after each other's children. There are several associations which can help (see Chapter 13), by putting you in touch with other single parents or with babysitters.

If you are having problems coping with your child, working, or just running the home you can always approach the social services. Social workers and health visitors are trained to help, and can suggest ways in which to alleviate the strain. They will know addresses of local playgroups, single-parent groups and so on which could relieve the pressure on you, or at least give you the chance to discuss your problems with people who have first-hand experience of them.

SCHOOL HOLIDAYS

The school holidays can be a strain, particularly first time round. You might not have enough money to take your children away on holiday, but they are quite likely to come back from school with stories about how so-and-so is going abroad, and so on. All you can do is explain to them gently that you cannot afford a proper holiday at present, and then give them as good a time as possible on the money available. They may well resent this at the time, and feel you are being a 'meany', or even cruel, but they will learn.

Even if money is short, you might be able to afford to send them off with friends on their family holiday, or to a camp organized by the school, or to stay with favourite relations.

You will also need to keep them busy at home. Try asking around locally. Some local authorities organize play schools, sports schemes and children's drama or music weekends in the holidays. Your child's teachers might also have some suggestions. (See Chapter 13.)

If you have problems with access at holiday-time, and you are finding it difficult to make a satisfactory arrangement with your former partner, you could approach a conciliation association to help you work something out.

If you are a working mother or father and find it difficult to take time off over the holiday period, and your ex cannot, or will not, have the children, try advertising locally for a temporary help. There will be a lot of students around at that time, many of whom will have had experience with children.

There are companies which organize holidays for children from the age of three upwards, but the holidays can be pricey. Some of the associations mentioned in Chapter 13 will advise on holiday camps, or organize holidays for children of single parents.

SCHOOL

It is important that your children are happy at school, especially if they are finding it difficult to come to terms with their new situation at home. If they can, and are happy to, stay at the same school, then so much the better. Teachers are usually very sympathetic in cases of separation or bereavement.

The child's teachers, headmaster or headmistress should be informed of the situation as soon as possible. They can watch the child to see if he is showing any sign of being seriously affected by the break-up or bereavement. Feel free to discuss with the teacher what can be done to help:

talking to another adult who knows your child will help take the strain off you.

If you are thinking of moving, it is important to check out the schools in the new area before you do so. You might prefer a school which is too far away from where you propose to live. It is better to find out before rather than after. Is the move really necessary? Consider your child's feelings about losing the friends he has made in his present school and home locality: is this a good time to deprive him of them?

Schools now have to publish information about themselves, and you should be able to get this free from the schools, a local library or the local education authority. If there is a Parent-Teacher Association, contact someone there to find out what the association thinks of the school and how it is run.

GETTING AWAY FROM THE CHILDREN

It is quite common for single parents to feel resentment towards their children or wish they did not have them at all. If you do feel like that from time to time, you have no reason to feel guilty. But take it as a warning sign.

If pressure is building up, you must find some way of dealing with it. If you cannot do it on your own you must get help from the professionals or your friends. Maybe getting away from the children for a short while is all that you need to do.

As Valerie, a divorcee of 32, explained: 'At first I resented my children, but looking back I now realize that they gave me the strongest purpose and reason to go on, to make a new life for us all. If I had not had to look after them I know I would never have made the effort to get back to living again. I could have given in so easily.'

Not only do your children need you, but you need them.

CHAPTER 9

Social life

When you become single after years of being part of a couple, the last thing you may feel like is socializing. You might feel you do not want to see anyone, which may be fine for a short while, but you have got to start living your life again. You may wish to see people, to talk to them, to relate to them, but you just cannot bring yourself to do so. You may be feeling low and need time to work out where you want to go and who you are. Maybe you cannot face explaining your situation to others. Although all this is understandable, you have to come to terms and accept it. You are going to have to make an effort some time.

Philippa, a young divorcee with a daughter, felt she needed to find new friends after the break rather than keeping up with old ones: 'We had been bickering and arguing for some time. We were forever "not talking to each other". My daughter who was then four was aware of what was going on and it was affecting her. Really I was very glad when we finally split.

'We had many friends when we were together, but I really didn't want to have to explain to them what had happened, to go over the past years or be reminded of him, and anyway they were my husband's friends, not mine. I dropped most of my own friends when we married. So I just wanted to start again. I have seen very few people from the old days since my husband left. And I have found it far easier and more satisfying to make new friends who don't know what happened in the past, and are prepared to get to know and like me for myself.'

SOCIALIZING WITHOUT YOUR PARTNER

At first you may find it difficult to socialize because you have relied on your partner for so many years that you feel unable to cope on your own in company.

Jo, an intelligent woman in her fifties who through her

job was well used to socializing with people on her own, recalled: 'After his death I was asked to attend a business "do" being held by his old firm. I suddenly felt terribly ill at ease at the idea of going all on my own. After all, it was his firm and I had always been to that sort of thing with my husband. I plucked up the courage to go, but when I arrived I had this overwhelming feeling that they were all looking at me, thinking "Why is she still alive, and not Tom?" I thought they just felt resentment at my being there. I understood their feelings, but it was something I had not been prepared for.'

Sally, a confident 40-year-old who had been married for twenty years, found large gatherings difficult to cope with: 'I was never particularly shy, but after my husband left I found it nearly impossible to go to any public function, or even friends' parties, on my own. I suppose I had got so used to my husband being there, to turn to if I got cornered by somebody I didn't like, to take me home, to talk about the people we had met. I realized that through him I was confident. Without him I felt like a fish out of water.'

If this is how you feel, the first priority is to gain confidence in yourself *as a whole person*, as someone who is capable of sharing thoughts, emotions and conversation with others, of giving and taking from other people; to believe in yourself and in what you can offer.

When you have been with someone for a long period of time, or have been under the influence of a parent, employer or dominant partner, you get used to being told what to do or think. Sometimes, if you have not previously ever been asked what you want or how you feel, it takes time to adjust to having to think on your own.

It is too easy to ask someone else's opinion and to rely on his or her judgement without making the effort of thinking for yourself. It makes life so much simpler to agree with someone rather than to stand up for what you want. This may be an easy way out, but it is not the right avenue for complete happiness or understanding of yourself.

Have you been relying solely on other people to make decisions? Do you know what you really want out of life? Do you have any opinions about issues of the day? If you are interested in things going on around you (not just locally, but globally as well), if you think about things, if you have opinions and views, not only will you find it easier to communicate with other people, but they will find you more interesting and attractive.

WORKING AT FRIENDSHIP

If you have suffered a bereavement or been through a separation, you may find it very difficult to admit to yourself initially that the situation you are in has even occurred. Once you have learnt to accept that it has, you will be able to get on with living life to the full again.

Cloistering yourself away like a hermit might be all right for a short time while you take stock and re-charge, but eventually you will have to make an effort to pick up the pieces. And remember, if you forget or reject your friends, they will eventually forget you.

Of course it is hard, when you are feeling low, to keep up human contact. People often mistakenly think that friends will not want to see them in their current state. But friendship goes far beyond a plus-and-minus balance sheet: your friends have to put up with sides of your character they may not like, and you have to do the same. Without give and take a friendship is worth nothing.

Friends who are only fair-weather friends are no friends at all. But they may be enjoyable acquaintances to pick up again when you feel stronger. If you go to see somebody who cheers you up, albeit temporarily, those few moments of feeling good will have considerable healing power.

Many people make the mistake of waiting for their friends or neighbours to make the first move, to invite them round for coffee, a drink or a meal. It is very likely that they will in the first few months, but thereafter it is up to you to make the return move. Just asking someone in for a cup of coffee or tea shows you are prepared to make the effort. It is not easy, but it has to be done.

Susan, who had many friends when her husband was alive, said she felt an outcast as a single person, and she lost contact with nearly all the people she knew. 'Friends asked me round three or four times on my own, but then the invitations tailed off. They just didn't seem to want someone without a partner. I tried asking them back, but they always suggested bringing a spare man they knew. I didn't want to meet single men. I suppose they just thought they were doing their best for the wife of a friend who had died.'

Unfortunately it is a fact of life that you cannot rely on

others forever. It has to be you who makes your new life, who makes the effort to retrench and start again.

NEW FRIENDS, OLD FRIENDS

You may have found that the friends on whom you thought you could rely have disappeared and perversely the ones you have only regarded as acquaintances have turned out to be marvellously supportive. But remember, there are always people out there who like you and want to help.

If you have been widowed, some people you know will find it so hard to deal with another person's grief that they just turn away, or cross the road to the other side if they see you. They do this not because they do not want to see you, but because they do not know what to say.

If you are separated or divorced, friends will very often take sides, which can cause you to lose possibly even good friends; otherwise, the situation can often put strain between you and them if they are not sure what to do. For this reason it is not at all surprising to find that five years after becoming single your circle of friends is completely different from the one you had before.

Charles, who divorced after ten years of marriage, found himself friendless. He explained why: 'When I married I gave up all my old bachelor friends, because my wife didn't get on with any of them, male or female. We moved to a new area and made a new set. When we divorced, all our friends seemed to side with my wife, and although I only moved a mile away from our old home I suddenly found I had no friends at all. So I moved to London, and for the third time I am beginning to make a new circle of friends. I now realize the value of keeping up contacts, and I won't make the same mistake again if I re-marry.'

Sheila, divorced at 36 with two boys, used to live in a tiny country village. 'The people in the village were marvellous when I was first on my own,' she recalled. 'They helped me with my children, they did shopping for me, they always chatted to me in the street. Six months later I met someone else, and as soon as they realized I was having a go at making a new life for myself they dropped me like a stone. It seemed extraordinary, because they had all spent hours telling me not to worry . . . one day I would fall in love again. Nobody talked to me. They even left the shop as I entered. I was an outcast. Maybe they thought I didn't need them any more, or perhaps they didn't approve of my new man. I just don't know.'

Sometimes you can be offered the wrong sort of friendship. This was the problem encountered by Marian, a divorced woman of 28: 'My social life plummeted,' she admitted, 'because wives invited me for tea with their kids, instead of dinner with adults.'

David, a divorced man of 35, also had problems: 'My friends certainly treated me differently. I didn't seem to get invited to their houses or to parties so often. And a lot of them treated me as though I had a terminal illness.'

THE 'COUPLE' SYNDROME

For all the increase in the number of single people – only one-third of the population of Britain falls into the 'family' category – there still seems to be a stigma attached to those who are not part of a couple.

Marcus, divorced at 28, experienced this problem, but knew it was not his fault: 'I wish my friends had said less, and behaved naturally. I didn't feel different towards them; I hadn't done anything wrong; I just wasn't part of a couple any longer. It took about a year for them to be normal, even apologize for being so awful.'

Jean, a widow of 45, found it took time to establish herself as an individual: 'My husband was much more extrovert than me and I tended to be in his shadow. Now my friends accept me as a person, rather than as a lesser part of a couple. And I know some of the women envy me and are a bit wary of me. I've got my independence – they haven't.'

People are reluctant to ask a single person to a dinner party. And if they do they invariably invite someone of the opposite sex to make up the numbers. Mostly all this achieves is to make the single people feel uncomfortable and wary of accepting invitations in the future. There is a lot of paranoia about making up numbers. When you give a party, do not make the same mistake.

John, in his thirties and recently separated, became aware that he was 'making up numbers' for friends: 'After we separated my friends were marvellous; they were always asking me round. My social life was excellent. But I realized after a time that they were asking me not because they really wanted my company, but because I was useful. I chatted to everyone, I poured the drinks, helped with the washing-up and was used as a partner for a variety of their single girlfriends, when the last thing I wanted was to be paired off with anyone.'

Christine, a separated woman of 32, became an object of envy to her female friends: 'Friends are wary of you because they are insecure in their own relationship. Women were envious of me. I found jealousy from women, but not from men. Some said to me: "Of course, you expected too much. Why weren't you content with your children? What more did you want? You had a husband, a house, etc." Basically they wanted to do it themselves.'

ENTERTAINING

Perhaps you have reached the stage where you are ready to return some of the kindness people have shown to you in your predicament and feel that the best way would be to invite them to your home. If you have never had to entertain single-handed before, some guidelines could be useful.

For most informal gatherings it is far easier to keep to one type of alcoholic drink, plus some soft drinks. Wine is the most acceptable all-purpose drink, and it is usually as well to allow about half to three-quarters of a bottle per person. Alternatively, you could make a wine cup – which can be as innocuous or as potent as you wish. It is always worth having some cans of lager or beer standing by as well: regular beer-drinkers may consume up to six pints a head. If serving spirits, allow about a quarter of a bottle per head and remember that you will need mixers – tonics, bitter lemons, ginger ale – as well.

Midday parties are usually shorter than evening drinks parties and people tend not to drink so much at that time of day, so you can assume a little less will be required.

In all cases you should have some soft drinks, for drivers, for those who do not drink alcohol, and for those who prefer to go on to something non-alcoholic after one or two alcoholic drinks.

It is better to over-provide rather than run short. Shop around your local off-licences and supermarkets for the best prices and deals.

Cocktail parties, usually starting in the early evening, can be great fun, but if you spend all your time mixing and serving drinks you will have little opportunity to talk to your guests. And there is no point giving a party which everyone enjoys except you.

Bear in mind that many off-licences will now take back up to 25 per cent of the drink you buy if it is not opened and will provide glasses free of charge (you pay only for breakages).

When serving drinks, it is a good idea to have a central table or particular room – like the kitchen – where the drink is laid out for people to help themselves, which will free you from having to worry about whether people have got drinks or not.

It is usually as well to provide something to eat at drinks parties – as simple yet as interesting as possible. Crisps and savoury biscuits with easily-made dips always make good staple nibbles. Sausages, which you can cook the night before, and fresh French bread with unusual cheeses, are also good standbys.

For more substantial food, supermarkets now sell very good frozen pizzas and quiches, and your local delicatessen may be a treasury of pâtés, cheeses, salads and cold meats. Looking round the shops will probably give you several new ideas. If you buy party food that you, and, if applicable, your children, like, at least the leftovers should not be too much of a problem.

If you are giving a full-scale dinner party, aim to provide both a balanced meal and a relaxed atmosphere. A simple stew with fresh bread and salad can be just as enjoyable as a six-course *nouvelle cuisine* extravaganza – the preparation of which has probably reduced you to an exhausted wreck.

Food does not have to be complicated to be enjoyable. However, do not forget that many people have voracious appetites: do provide enough.

Talk to your butcher, fishmonger, or greengrocer before you buy. They will advise you on quantities and, if you ask, the best way to cook it as well.

Try to balance the tastes and flavours of your meal. No one wants to eat three courses of over-rich food, or of very similar food. If you are inviting people to dinner that you do not know very well, find out first whether they have any particular dislikes.

If you have a vegetarian or vegan coming to dinner, cook something especially for him or her which will fit in with what everyone else is having, and likewise if you are vegetarian and you have a meat-eater coming for a meal.

Before you start, work out how long each item is going to take to cook and prepare as much as you can in advance. It is only lack of thought, not lack of ability, that causes a quarter-hour wait for the vegetables when the meat is ready and rapidly cooling.

Above all, allow yourself enough time. If you are hosting the occasion on your own, you can hardly leave your guests on their own while you disappear to peel the potatoes. But if things do not go quite according to plan, do not get flustered. Ask one of your guests to help. No one will mind. If you enjoy yourself, so will everyone else.

If you are nervous about giving your first dinner party single-handed, try a 'dry run' with one friend.

HOLIDAYS

Most people do not look forward to taking a holiday on their own. If you are young, you may have single friends you can go with, or know of groups which you can join in. Otherwise, several companies specialize in holidays for single people, with or without their children, both in Britain and abroad. Several singles organizations have holiday schemes (see Chaper 13). Alternatively, remember that a good travel agent will either find or put together a package to suit you, working to a pre-arranged budget.

One of the joys of holidaying alone is that you never know whom you might meet. You could be lucky enough to find some people in a similar situation as yourself, or just people with whom you get on well. Even if the trip does not work out as you expected, look on it as an experiment, one to learn from. If nothing else, it will have taken you out of the house and your routine, which is most important.

Diana, who is 29 and separated, had never been on holiday alone before, and faced the experience with some trepidation. 'As a kid,' she explained, 'I always went with my parents, then girlfriends, then my husband. The thought of booking something when I didn't know anyone else on the holiday horrified me. But I desperately needed a break. A friend was enthusing about a mini-cruise she had been on – how great the people were, what fun it was – and I woke up one morning thinking, "It's now or never, I've got to do something."

'So I went to a travel agent . . . and booked a five-day

cruise to Denmark. I felt very nervous when I arrived, I nearly turned back when I saw everyone else going on board. But I made it. There was a welcoming party the first evening and the purser made sure no one was left out. I had a smashing time, and next year I'm going again, this time with two of the girls I met on the trip.'

If your budget allows, you could go to a health farm for a week. Toning the body can also help tone the mind, and such a holiday would certainly give you a complete break from routine. One recommendation came from Susan, a 45-year-old divorcee: 'A week at a health farm rejuvenates me in body and mind. I feel strong enough to face any problem afterwards. I look and feel better – feel more confident in myself because I know I look better. It does me the world of good. I've also made some good friends.'

If you are energetic and can spare the time, what about a working holiday? You could take a week or a month, either in the UK or abroad, and perhaps visit places you would not otherwise be able to afford. More specific information on these holidays is provided in Chapter 13 and the Bibliography.

An older person going on holiday alone may find it a bit more of a problem. If you are working you could try to organize a trip for a group of people in your company. You might well find there are quite a few people who have been looking for just such an opportunity. Some of your friends may be in the same position, too.

You could try a specialist holiday, incorporating a hobby or interest you particularly enjoy: riding, painting, flower-arranging, yoga, cooking, accountancy, furniture restoration, ornithology – the possibilities now on offer are very wide-ranging. (See Bibliography.)

Making new friends is not easy for anyone, whether single or not. But the more chances you give yourself to meet people the more likely you are to find people whose company you enjoy. You cannot make friends by shutting yourself up at home feeling sorry for yourself.

CHAPTER 10

Homosexual relationships

Although much of the advice and information throughout this book applies to homosexuals as well as heterosexuals, this chapter covers some of the specific problems encountered by homosexuals.

When a homosexual couple breaks up, or when one partner dies, the problems and pain experienced are for the most part the same as those faced by heterosexual couples. But there are also pressures, because the attitudes of other people towards gays differ and can often make the situation harder to come to terms with.

Sometimes it is not even other people's attitudes but your own that are making things difficult. Because you are reluctant to be honest about your situation, other people are reluctant to talk about it when a problem occurs. They may know and want to help, to sympathize, to offer words of comfort, but how can they when they are not meant to know?

Peter found himself in this situation. He explained: 'I had been living with Simon for seven years. We had not broadcast the fact we were gay because we both had very good jobs in banking and if our employers had known we would have probably been sacked. So when Simon died suddenly, after a car accident, I found it difficult, in fact impossible, to talk to anyone about the loss I really felt. Not only had I lost a good friend but also my lover. We had never got involved in the gay scene – it didn't really appeal to us – so I couldn't even turn to other gays.

'Five years later I still found myself bursting into tears in the most unexpected places and in embarrassing situations. I eventually went to a psychologist who explained that because I had never been able to grieve properly for my love, I had suppressed it and it was bursting inside me, trying to get out.'

It took two more years for Peter to come to terms with the

grief and to make a new life for himself.

PROMISCUITY

For a myriad of reasons there is a high proportion of promiscuity in gay relationships and, as a result, few relationships last a long time. Not being monogamous has both good and bad effects. It can mean that when you are deserted (or you leave someone) you have other people to whom you can turn. On the other hand, you might find that even your own circle of friends fails to provide the sympathy that you need.

BEREAVEMENT

One immediate practical problem is that bereaved homosexuals who are employed are not allowed time off work (unless their boss is very understanding) in the same way that married partners are.

Emotionally, too, homosexuals often carry an extra burden. Their grieving process can be made more difficult and slower to work through because they cannot be as open about it as they would like, and because other people find it difficult to comprehend their suffering.

In the period immediately following the death of a partner, they may well find that their partner's family is hostile, even if the family knew and was happy about the situation when the son or daughter was alive. Now that he or she is dead, the family's attitudes may completely change. You may know, for example, that your partner would have liked a particular type of burial or form of funeral service. But the family has the right to decide on the arrangements, and whatever you say may go unheeded.

Jane recalled her experience after her partner's death: 'I still remember the pain at Maria's funeral. It was not the family's fault. They knew of our relationship and were quite happy about it. They had agreed that my bunch of red roses should be put on the coffin rather than theirs. But just before the service the undertaker noticed the wreath on the coffin was not from her parents. So he removed my flowers and replaced it with the family's wreath.'

The hurt of that incident – an innocent mistake – has stayed in Jane's mind ever since.

At the funeral, the clergy conducting the service may ignore the existence of a homosexual partner – either because they do not approve, or because they are unaware of the situation. The service will then be directed towards the family, and quite often you will find the lover – the one most important and closest to the deceased – at the back of the church, not being able, or allowed, to show respect in the way he or she would like.

It is therefore important to make sure before the funeral that the undertaker and the clergy understand the situation.

Plenty of gay couples live together keeping up the pretence to outsiders that they are 'just good friends'. Neighbours who would normally call round, on hearing of a bereavement, to offer their help and their sympathies find it difficult to do so if they do not understand the relationship. Do not be afraid to explain the true situation to neighbours or 'straight' friends. There are far more people who will help you and be sympathetic to you as an individual – regardless of their views on homosexuality in general – than you might think.

It is vitally important for gay couples to make wills, for although you are living as a married couple, because you are not one there is no financial protection for the surviving partner. If no will is made, everything the deceased owned will automatically go to the next of kin as stipulated in law. Even if a will has been made, the surviving relations may contest it, and unfortunately when this happens often the partner does not fight back because of the unwanted attention it attracts.

If you live with someone as a 'marriage partner' it might be worth going to see a solicitor and working out legal ways of giving yourselves legal protection in the event of one of you dying.

Georgie, who is 61, lost her lover seven years ago and was badly hurt by the conduct of her partner's unthinking, insensitive relations at a time when she most needed love and support: 'I married very young and had two children, a daughter and a son. I was pretty ignorant about my sexuality then, but soon realized things were not right with the marriage and it broke down. Because we felt we could not jeopardize our children's lives, we decided to stay together – in that we would share the same roof and expenses. We still live in the same house. We tolerate each other now, but that is all.

'I had been with Marjorie for twenty-two years, and her death was very sudden. She had gone to her parents over Christmas, and while she was there she was going to put all our photographs kept over the years into an album – to give to me when she returned after the break.

'She died there, and although her family knew about our relationship they would not recognize it. And because of that they didn't tell me of her death straight away. When they rang, they just said: "She's dead. And there is no way you will get the photographs. They have been burnt. What you did to our daughter was wicked. You destroyed her."

'As you can imagine, this caused me so much pain, at a time when I was absolutely distraught and when I was least able to deal with such hurt. I couldn't go to the funeral, because I didn't know when it was. It was all very traumatic.

'My children were as supportive as they could be, but they never really understood. They had grown up knowing about our relationship, but they cannot understand that it is the same as being husband and wife; they just cannot conceive it means as much. Certainly none of my straight friends could. A woman at work just said, "You can always masturbate". What a deeply insensitive and negative statement!

'I felt tremendous insecurity, suddenly finding myself on my own. It was very bad news, and I was very aware of having no one to turn to. Six months after Marjorie's death, I was still very low and finding it difficult to get back into life, especially having nobody to really talk to.

'I ran into a mutual friend – a gay man – and blurted it all out. He understood my grief, what I was going through, and what it meant to me. We walked and cuddled, and he gave me the support I had needed all those months back.

'Then I joined a homosexual group which has been marvellously helpful.'

It is also important to remember that if your partner goes into hospital he or she should name you as the next of kin. Then, if visiting or information has to be limited to family only, as can often happen, you will not be denied access.

This happened to Colin: 'When Barry was ill I rang [the hospital] several times a day to find out how he was. When they discovered I was not a member of the family they became less helpful. When he was transferred to the intensive care department they told me nothing at all. It was only when Barry's mother, who knew the situation, intervened that I was allowed to visit him.'

If you are religious, then many – but, of course, not all – clergy will be happy to talk, help and give advice. Many gays – whether bereaved or separated – have said that the Church has provided a great deal of help, besides being somewhere to go to discuss problems. Religious belief has given them strength.

BREAKING UP
When a heterosexual loses a partner he or she can talk to friends, relations and colleagues. These people may not react in the right way, but at least they will be able to imagine and understand the suffering.

In the case of homosexuals – men or women – this is less likely. Even if you have been open about your sexuality, straight colleagues and friends will often find it harder to understand. If the partnership has been kept secret, the situation will be even worse.

For example, if you, as a gay man, have been living with a guy but have not 'come out', and your partner walks out on you, you will feel distraught, desperately unhappy, lonely, rejected. But to outsiders the person who has gone was just a friend. They cannot understand why you should be so upset. Because they did not know the true situation, you cannot talk to them, or let your feelings go to the outside world. You have to bottle up those feelings and pretend everything is OK.

It is important to find a release, to work through your feelings and to let them out. There are clubs and associations that can help (see Chapter 13).

Even if you have been open about being gay, splitting up with your partner is still deeply stressful. Alan, 41, told a familiar story – of not being able to recover from the break-up until he could confide in someone else completely: 'I had been with James for eight and a half years. We met at ballet school when I was 22. Although this was my first relationship, I had known since I was nine that I didn't fancy girls, and when I was older I realized I was gay. Because I had been aware of my feelings for such a long time, I just accepted the way I was.

'I had a big family, two sisters and three brothers, who all knew. My parents knew too, although we never actually spoke about it. When I was with James they treated him like a son-in-law, and his parents did the same with me. It was just never actually discussed.

'James lived in the north of England, and I was based in London. After several years of only seeing each other at weekends, I decided to give up my career and move to be with him. At the time I thought the relationship would last for ever. But it got fraught. He was working and was away a lot. We just didn't seem to see enough of each other. I went abroad for a year, and came back thinking we could make things work. But it was just the same. After eight and a half years I moved back to London. I didn't want to leave James, but I knew it had to be done.

'Although it is ten years ago I still think about him every day. I still love him, and although I have had other relationships, they have not meant as much.

'It took me about nine years to be able to talk about it. My parents were very supportive, but when I came back to London, I was 30 and all alone . . .

'I was very lonely, and didn't know whom to turn to. There were friends who were very sweet and helpful, but they all had their own lives to lead. It didn't help that my mother had a stroke and died eight weeks afterwards, and my father died nine months later. I almost completely broke down. . .

'The person who helped me most was my priest. He is so understanding. I have been able to talk to him and he has given me strength.'

If you need some support because you are now on your own, remember that as well as the specifically gay associations and groups that have been set up to help people in such a position you can also contact a marriage guidance bureau: these deal not only with relationships that are breaking up, but those suffering from the after-effects of a break-up, including homosexual as well as heterosexual couples.

GENERAL ASSISTANCE
Whether you are suffering from loneliness or an inability to cope, are worried about your sexuality and feelings of isolation, or have a simple practical problem, such as where to live, the gay help lines and counselling services are

extremely efficient, and always willing to help in any way they can. However, bear in mind that many can only be contacted in the evenings.

The message for bereaved or separated homosexuals seems to be exactly the same as for everyone else: it takes time to work through the grief and pain of loss, but what seems to help most is human contact – reaching out to others.

CHAPTER 11

Practicalities

Quite often it is the practical aspects of being left on their own that fill people with fear. There may be bills and taxes to be paid, other financial matters to be sorted out; major decisions to be taken alone – whether to move house, and perhaps, if you move to another area, which school to send your child to; whether to get a new car; petty annoyances, such as a leaking tap, to attend to. The list can seem endless.

The first thing to do is to sit down and take stock. Make yourself lists of everything you are worried about or you think needs doing. Then sort them into order of importance. Having things down on paper makes them so much easier to deal with, and it is much better than letting them go round and round in circles in your mind.

Take things slowly: set yourself targets which you can manage, and you will feel good at getting each thing, however small, done. Try to do one job at a time.

Olivia, who was widowed in her early sixties, found this was the only way she could get to grips with life: 'I found it so hard to concentrate on anything, to get anything done I wanted to. I felt I was never going to be able to do all the thousands of things that had to be done, and consequently didn't get any of them done. Because of this I felt more useless, more incapable and in utter despair.

'One morning I wrote down a few things I wanted to do that day – clean out the fridge, move the picture in the hall to the bedroom, which I had been meaning to do for months, pick the vegetables in the garden. At the end of the day I had managed to do them. Some people might not think it was very impressive, but it made me feel so much better.'

Olivia was wrong when she says people will not find what she did impressive. People do not expect as much of us as we sometimes imagine. Of course what she did was impressive: at last Olivia was starting what was probably to be a long haul to recovery. Remember, you cannot expect to reach the summit of the Matterhorn in one step.

If there is anything you cannot cope with, ask friends or neighbours. You will be surprised how much people love to be asked to help with something: so often the response is, 'If only you had asked me sooner, I would have been round like a shot.' If you wait for somebody to offer you might be waiting a long time, but it does not mean people do not want to help: it is more probable that they are nervous about intruding on your grief.

Joanna, a widow of 55, found a lot of practical support on her own doorstep: 'I relied on tradesmen more than my friends in the first few months – the jobbing gardener, the man who was painting the house next door and the plumber down the road all helped me enormously. My friends supported me emotionally, but the practical jobs flummoxed me. I could not have managed without the removal man who helped me move house and the people who found markets for things I wanted to sell.'

There is nothing wrong with making use of other people who can help with the problems we cannot solve, and in many cases it just takes a little concerted effort to learn how to do something. It is all too easy to say, 'I've never done this before, so I can't possibly learn now.' It is *never* too late to learn.

RUNNING THE HOME ON YOUR OWN

Many people find it very difficult to live in the home they shared with their partner, particularly if they have been bereaved. Memories keep flooding back, and they find themselves doing the same things as they did before, without really thinking. Yet as soon as they can start to alter their lifestyle they will be moving forward and learning to live on their own.

Making changes certainly marked a starting-point for Jane, a middle-aged widow: 'I think it is a big mistake to keep doing all the same things you have been doing all your life. I was miserably drifting through my days after my husband died, doing things for both of us – but there was only me. I didn't want to move. I loved our house. A friend suggested I repaint the whole house. I was well provided for, so I got in some decorators. I never realized how much work I would have to do and it kept me involved for weeks. I didn't have time to be miserable.

'When it was finished I felt as if a huge weight had been lifted from my shoulders. I felt like a new person, and I suddenly realized that the colours I had chosen for the rooms were colours my husband wouldn't have approved of. It was almost like my subconscious was making me turn over a new leaf, so that I could get on with my new life.'

Wendy, a young widow whose husband, an artist, had died suddenly, recalled her reluctance to disturb his personal working environment: 'I wouldn't go near his studio and I wouldn't let my cleaning lady touch it. One day a friend who was putting together an exhibition of his work went into the studio, only to find a very mouldy fruit bowl which was almost walking on its own and an evil-looking half-finished cup of coffee. I had to laugh and vowed to tidy the studio up the next day.'

If you have been bereaved, you will eventually have to sort out the deceased's clothes and give them away. This may be difficult to do in the first few very painful months, but should be attempted as soon as you feel stronger. It is no good hanging on the past, although a few keepsakes will of course be of comfort for years afterwards.

Valerie, who was widowed at 49, found it helped to keep something her husband had worn close by her: 'When my husband passed away I sat holding his slippers close to me. I kept them with me for quite a few days, until I knew I just had to let go and come to terms with my new life. I have now put the slippers away.'

Another widow, Joan, aged 45, described what she did with her husband's clothing: 'As soon as I felt strong enough to sort out his clothes, I went through them and gave away most of them. I gave all his underwear and pyjamas to people who needed them. I enjoyed feeling I was helping other people out, and I knew John would have been happy about it.

'I wear his trousers, his shirts and socks for gardening. People may think I am odd, but why not? It doesn't upset me, and I feel they are being put to good use. The only clothes I haven't got rid of are his Crombie overcoat and dinner-jacket, and the only reason I haven't is because I couldn't find the right person to give them to. I will if that person comes along.'

BUDGETING

Never a truer word has been spoken than by Charles Dickens' character Mr Micawber in *David Copperfield*:

'Annual income £20, annual expenditure £19 19s 6d: result happiness.

'Annual income £20, annual expenditure £20 0s 6d: result misery.'

If you have never had to budget before, now is the time to start. Figures are not as frightening as they might seem at first. Who knows, you might even get to like them!

The secret is to be organized and to work out your full expenditure; do not cheat on yourself, because you will only end up with less money than you bargained for. For example, if you would like to cut down on cigarettes, but cannot manage it at the moment, it is no good allowing for expenditure on 20 a day when you know that you are more likely to smoke 30.

Make a list of all fixed-amount bills: rent, rates, mortgage. Then list the other essentials, such as food, heating, electricity, gas, clothing, travel, car. What is left can be spent on non-essential items such as drink, cigarettes, entertaining, holidays, and the occasional luxury. If possible, try to put some money aside for savings, too.

If you are having difficulty paying the mortgage, rent or rates you might be able to get help from the social services (see Chapter 12).

If you do not know where to start, go and see your bank manager, who will help you sort out your budget plans and will suggest the best way to manage your money – however much or little you have. The Citizens' Advice Bureau will also advise on money difficulties.

ECONOMIES

Now you are on your own, there may be less money coming in, and you may have to start making some economies, particularly if the breadwinner of the partnership is no longer around.

Economizing does not mean being a martyr, or not being able to enjoy your life. It is all about fitting what you want to do into your new financial situation. You will be surprised at how much money you can save through very simple economies.

Work out what you actually want and what you do not

really care about: with forward planning, you should be able to find a way of covering essentials and having some money to fall back on in emergency.

You might have to change some of your habits. Do you, for instance, pick up the phone whenever you feel like talking to someone? If so, you could cut your phone bill by ringing people only at off-peak times. If there is someone you talk to regularly who is better off than you, do not feel embarrassed about asking him or her to phone you sometimes instead of the other way round.

What about your shopping trips into town? By planning ahead and making fewer trips you could save money on petrol or fares.

If you are worried about heating costs, put on more clothing, rather than the heating, if you are going to be in a room only for a short while. A pleasant temperature for a living-room is 20 degrees centigrade. By dropping this by 1 degree, you could save 5 per cent on your heating bill. And what about those draughts around your home? They are costing you money.

Turn the heating off at night. Once you are tucked up in bed, more bedclothes, warmer nightwear or a hot-water bottle are cheaper than all-night heating (but remember, of course, that old people and people with young babies must be very careful not to skimp on heating).

If you have a problem with making ends meet, see whether the social services can help.

Do not accept things as they are. Check them out. Cecily did, to her advantage. 'I pay for my central heating oil by standing order once a month,' she explained. 'A friend saw one of my bills and told me she was paying 5p less a unit than I was. So I rang up my company and told them I could get cheaper oil elsewhere. They immediately agreed to reduce my bill. I must have saved myself about £50.'

Talk to staff of the relevant organization (electricity, gas, solid fuel) about how to save on your fuel bills (see Chapter 13).

HOUSEHOLD CHORES

There are probably many household tasks that you relied on your partner to do. Now, there is no earthly reason why you should not learn to do them for yourself.

John, a young divorcee, had always expected his wife to

shop, cook and wash up, but had to face these tasks alone after the break-up: 'Looking back, it was pretty bloody silly, but the first time I went out on a Saturday to shop for myself I felt frightened, lost and didn't know what to buy. The next weekend I dragged along my poor, long-suffering secretary around the shops to help me. Once I got into it I couldn't understand why people make such a fuss – it is a doddle.'

The stereotyping of roles is just one more thing that creates problems when couples split up. Both sexes can do any job in the house, equally well.

Simon, who has had to fend for himself for some time now, found that cooking could help him unwind: 'I find it extremely relaxing after a hard day's work to come home to cook. I can chop vegetables while listening to the radio, or sorting things out in my mind, invent and create different dishes, and if it doesn't work, well, there's only myself to please, and I can always start again.'

Ingrid, widowed for just two months, was suddenly confronted by a common household emergency: 'I was in the house by myself one evening when suddenly all the lights went out. I panicked. I didn't know what had happened, I thought there must have been a power cut. I didn't even know where the fuse-box was. I rang a neighbour, and luckily he came straight over.

'The first thing he asked me was whether I had a trip switch. I had never heard of such a thing. Eventually he found it – I have since learnt that this is a safety measure which stops the whole electrical circuit blowing – and with a flip of the switch the lights came on. I did feel stupid.

'We found the faulty machine (it was the toaster), and I now make sure I keep a torch handy, know where the fuse-box is, as well as the trip switch, and how to change a fuse.'

If such tasks are completely unfamiliar to you, read about coping with them before you have an emergency on your hands. There are books giving detailed information on how to change fuses and light bulbs, do simple repairs, and so on (see Bibliography).

SHOPPING
There are a few basic rules to remember while shopping. Make a list of what you want, stick to it and do not be tempted by special offers of items which you do not need.

Shops make a lot of extra money out of people who buy more than they really want.

Street markets are the cheapest place to buy food, especially late in the day; stall-holders do not want produce going bad on them, so they will reduce their prices. If you have the nerve, try a bit of bargaining.

Supermarkets are always cheaper than small local shops, and can, for those on a tight budget, make a tremendous difference; but if you have to travel twenty miles to a supermarket, that is a different matter. Do your sums. The petrol or travel costs might eat up whatever you have saved in the store.

Buy fresh food as often as you can. Not only is it better for you, it is invariably cheaper than tinned or frozen food. It might take slightly longer to prepare, but it is worth the effort. If you are not sure about quantities, which cut of meat or type of vegetable or fish to buy, or how to cook it, ask someone, or have a browse through some cookbooks.

COOKING

Rule number one is to eat a regular, balanced diet. You might think that that statement is rather obvious, yet the number of people who do not eat properly is astounding. Many think that because they can keep going on junk food their diet is perfectly satisfactory. But later on in life they may well suffer from the years of surviving on an inadequate diet. Eating more sensibly will always bring benefits in terms of your general health and well-being.

How many times have you said, 'I don't feel like eating tonight', 'It's not worth cooking unless I have someone to cook for', 'I can't be bothered' or 'I am too busy to worry about food; anyway I've nothing in the house'?

There is no mystique about being able to cook. You need to be reasonably organized, have some kitchen scales and a few good cookery books, and to watch what you are doing. Most mistakes are made when you are not concentrating: leaving pans to boil dry, or not following the recipe properly. Read the recipe before you shop for the ingredients to get a rough idea of what you have to do. If you have not cooked before, start with simple recipes and then move on gradually (some useful books are listed in the Bibliography).

If money is not a problem, a freezer can be invaluable. It

means you can cook in bulk when you have the time. Once you have stocked the freezer, you have the satisfaction of knowing that when you are rushed there will always be something there. It also means you can buy fruit, vegetables, meat and fish when they are at their cheapest and their seasonal best. And if you have food left over – from a joint, or from a party – you can freeze it for later instead of throwing it away.

If you are short of space, an electric multi-cooker is a good buy. This is basically an electric frying-pan with a domed lid, and is more economical to run than a full-scale cooker. You can fry, grill, bake, boil and roast in the same pan, and you can plug it into an ordinary socket.

Another good idea for working people is the electric slow-cooker, which is useful for stews and casseroles. You put the ingredients into the casserole in the morning, turn it on, and when you get back from work in the evening a piping hot meal is ready and waiting for you. Alternatively, there is the pressure cooker, which cooks things at great speed. So, of course, does the microwave oven, which could be a worthwhile investment if you have a very busy life.

YOUR RIGHTS TO YOUR HOME
If you are not sure where you stand in respect of ownership of your home, consult a solicitor. Some pertinent points are listed below, and the Bibliography includes books that go into far greater detail on the subject.

If the matrimonial home is in your partner's name and he or she leaves you in it, it is quite possible that the home could be sold without your knowledge and you could find yourself homeless. If you think this is a possibility, you should immediately register your interest in the property (your solicitor will act for you).

In England and Wales, you can protect your rights to your home by asking your solicitor to make a Class F land charge. If your spouse should try to sell the property, this will automatically show up on the deeds, which will prevent any sale being made without your consent, or a court agreement.

If you are in rented property, and the property is rented in your spouse's name, there is little you can do to protect yourself – unless you are a sitting tenant, in which case the landlord will find it difficult to evict you.

You can apply for transfer of the property in divorce or judicial separation proceedings.

In Scotland you can put an inhibition on the house (similar to a Class F land charge) only in certain circumstances, such as your husband leaving the country or going bankrupt. This prevents the house being sold without some payment being made to you. If the home is rented, however, the tenancy can be transferred to your name. In a divorce settlement, you have the right to demand money, not property. This can be in the form of maintenance for yourself and any children, and a capital payment – which takes account of the marital home.

If you are cohabiting and the house is in your partner's name, you can apply to the court to declare that you have an equitable interest because you have paid for capital improvements, repairs, or a substantial amount of the mortgage repayments. After you have commenced proceedings you can register the pending action against the house, thus preventing its being sold or charged before your interest is determined. But this is a difficult case to establish. The easiest way, of course, to preserve your rights is to make sure your name is on the title deeds.

In the case of divorce between a couple with children, the court usually awards the mother the matrimonial home, unless she leaves of her own accord, on the premise that it is essential that the children have the security of a roof over their heads, and that it is far less upsetting for children to stay in the home in which they have been brought up than to be moved elsewhere.

In cases where a father has been left with the children, he will be awarded the home. Only about 12 per cent of fathers are given custody of their children. (Many men feel that the laws on divorce and custody settlements are unfairly biased towards women.)

If the divorce is not amicable, it is often advisable to see a marriage guidance counsellor or a conciliation service to help you work out a fair settlement for you and your children. It is far better if you can both agree to abide by an impersonal arbitrator's decision to sort out the answer than to try to sort the matter out yourselves when you are both distraught, angry and distressed.

As a widow or widower, if your home is in joint tenancy

(i.e. in both names) it automatically reverts to you. If it is owned by tenancy in common (i.e. you each owned one half of the home) you retain your part and the part owned by your partner will have to go through probate before it can be transferred to your name.

If the property is in your partner's name you will have to wait until probate is cleared before it is transferred to your name; this is done by a simple court order. Any mortgage will either have to be cleared (if there is an insurance policy), or you will have to transfer the mortgage. Building societies will usually allow payments to be held up for some time if you are waiting for probate, and are always helpful.

If there is a bank, council, building society or private mortgage on the property you must let the mortgagees know immediately of any change of circumstance.

WHETHER TO MOVE OR NOT

One of the great mistakes many people who are suddenly single make is to move home, or take the decision to uproot, far too soon. For several months, or even years, after the divorce or bereavement you will be in a most vulnerable state, and this is not the time to do something rash.

Instead, sit tight and wait until you are fit and ready to make rational decisions. It is so easy, for example, to think you want to live in the country if you have always been in the city, or the other way round. You might think: 'I've always dreamt of doing that, but I couldn't when I was married.' So you sell up, move to the new location, live there for six months and discover you hate it.

The problem is a common one, but hindsight usually produces the same conclusion, as summarized by Kathryn, who was widowed in late middle age. 'The one mistake I think widows must avoid is taking a panic decision to move house because of financial uncertainty. You can end up moving into the wrong house in the wrong place, not realizing that grief has distorted your view and under-mined your commonsense. Unfortunately several of my friends have done this and got themselves into an awful mess.'

If you wait until you are capable of thinking rationally you may discover that although you may have thought you wanted to live elsewhere, in reality it might have had drawbacks. You would perhaps be leaving behind much-needed friends and supportive neighbours, a job that was helping to keep you on an even keel, or, if you have children, you might have found that moving them from a school where they were settled to a new educational environment added greatly to their own emotional suffering. The very process of moving is in itself traumatic, too.

A widow named Anne had no doubts that hasty decisions were likely to be the wrong ones: 'I am firmly convinced that if finances allow you should stay put for as long as you are able, before making any decision which you may regret for the rest of your life. You may be in a turmoil, heartbroken – perhaps you cannot bear going into some rooms at all – and you wonder why you bother to go on. I was advised to sell my house within the year. I nearly took that advice, but couldn't do it. Later I was very thankful for not having made any rash decision. Five years on I am still here, and I am extremely grateful that I am.'

Another common mistake is to move in with relatives, especially parents. This may seem the ideal solution at first: for example, if you have young children, grandparents are often willing babysitters, which would mean you could have time to yourself. But it is more likely that you will get on top of each other. For a short period living with relatives could work, but it is very rarely a good long-term solution.

MOVING

So you have decided that you really want to move. You have waited long enough, thought hard about it and are sure you are making the right decision.

It is well worth spending some time in the area you want to move to if you do not already know it. Stay there for a couple of weekends, get to know some of the locals, talk to people in the post office, local shops or pubs. Ask around, find out what amenities are available, talk to estate agents and buy the local paper. Building societies, bank managers or the local authority will advise you on how much money you can borrow if you need a mortgage in order to buy your home. (See Chapter 12, and the Bibliography.)

Remember that even if you are turned down for a mortgage by one company, another may well be able to provide one. Their loan resources and their conditions for lending do vary.

If you are selling your home, ask a number of estate agents to look at the property and give their view on how much you can ask for it. Ask them what commission they would charge, but do not necessarily accept their figure. Many agents will lower their percentage if you query it.

If you do not have a solicitor, ask more than one what their conveyancing fees would be for a buying and selling transaction, and tell them you are asking around.

If you are moving house, you will probably need a removal firm to help you. This always needs some research, because charges, as well as service, vary enormously. Some firms will come the day before to wrap china and glass and on the day carefully pack everything into tea chests. And when they get to the other end they will put everything where you want it. But this sort of service costs money. Like most things in life, you get what you pay for. Others expect you to have everything packed, and they will just dump the crates in one room for you to sort out.

At the cheaper end of the scale are working drivers with vans who advertise in the local papers; they can often be a better bet than the professionals – but it is pot luck. If you have any friends in the vicinity who have moved home within the last few years, ask them whether the people they used were reliable. Either way, it is worth getting one or more friends round to help you. Do check what sort of insurance policy the removal people have. If necessary you can always take out an extra policy to cover your move. It is always better to be safe than sorry.

RENTED HOMES

If you rent your home and want to move you will have to give up your lease, having given the appropriate notice, and look round for a new tenancy. If you are already renting from the local authority, or housing association, there may be special schemes to help you.

For example, if you rent from a public landlord, ask whether you can be nominated for a move under the National Mobility Scheme (a leaflet about this scheme is available from local authority housing departments and the Citizens' Advice Bureaux). If so, you will have to fill in the relevant form giving, for example, proof of a job or job offer in the new area. In some large cities there is a mobility scheme within the area of that city.

You could also enquire from the local authority about the Tenants' Exchange Scheme, whereby you swop homes with a tenant in another council's area. There is no charge for using this scheme and you can get a registration form from the housing authority or local council. If a tenant who has seen details of your property is interested he will get in touch with you direct, or you can go to your housing department and look for reciprocal notices. Once you have agreed on a move you have to get written permission from your respective landlords.

A variety of leaflets and booklets about moving, housing grants and related subjects is available free from local authority housing departments and Citizens' Advice Bureaux.

Some towns have housing associations for unsupported mothers and their children which buy large houses and convert them into flats. Living in such an environment means you will almost always have a ready and understanding supply of babysitters, and you will be able to discuss experiences and viewpoints with people who are in a similar situation to you, which can be a great comfort. To find out about these flats, enquire at the local authority's housing department.

PAYING FOR THE HOME

If you are on supplementary benefit, or if your earnings are low and you are finding it difficult to pay your rates, rent, mortgage interest payments or heating you can get help (see chapter 12). Even if you are a single person without children or you rent your home there is help available. Get in touch with your local Department of Health and Social Security or the Citizens' Advice Bureau as soon as you can, and they will either advise you on how to apply for assistance or put you in touch with the relevant voluntary organizations for help.

If you are on supplementary benefit you might be able to claim removal expenses.

Renting

It is cheaper to rent unfurnished property, and if you have divided your old home you will probably have furniture which it is better to use than put into store. Alternatively, you could pick up second-hand furniture from sales and auctions.

Furnished accommodation now has the same security of tenure as unfurnished, and you can move in without having to worry about buying carpets, curtains, furniture and so on.

In either case, check whether you have to pay extra for the rates and whether there are any other extra outgoings for which will be responsible. Make sure you are given a rent book by your landlord, and that this is kept up to date.

If you think the rent you are being charged is too high, you can go to a rent officer, who, if he agrees with you, will refer the matter to a rent tribunal. You can get in touch with the rent officer at your local authority's offices.

Subletting
To help pay the bills you could sublet part of your home, but check first whether your mortgage or lease allows you to do so. Before entering into any contract it is a good idea to take legal advice. A Citizens' Advice Bureau or legal centre should be able to help.

Ask friends if they know of anyone who is looking for somewhere to live. If you put an advertisement in the paper or local shop window, make sure you have good references from would-be tenants.

A leaflet, *Letting Rooms in Your Home*, can be obtained from the housing department or a Citizens' Advice Bureau.

Buying a council house
If you have been a council tenant for three or more years, you can buy a council house. However, this does not necessarily mean the property you live in, or even one in the same area. The discount you will receive depends on how long you have been a tenant, and ranges from 33 per cent to a maximum of 50 per cent. Apply to the local housing department if you are interested.

SOLICITORS
If you are widowed, you will probably already have a family solicitor whom you can continue to consult and who could well be a source of strength and help to you not only in the case of legal matters but also of financial and personal problems.

If you are getting legally separated or divorced, you may wish to find a different solicitor from the one your partner is using (however, this is not necessary and the operation will be cheaper and easier if you are both happy to use the same solicitor).

First of all, ask friends for recommendations. This is usually the easiest and surest way of finding a good solicitor. But bear in mind that many solicitors specialize in a particular subject, so just because he was marvellous in your friend's libel case, or did a good conveyancing job, or helped someone in the fight to recover some money, it does not necessarily mean the same solicitor will be a brilliant divorce lawyer.

You can write to the Law Society (see Chapter 13), but although it will provide a list of solicitors in your area it will not give recommendations. If you are having trouble finding a solicitor your bank manager or accountant should be able to recommend one.

Once you have found the name of a solicitor, make an appointment and see him first for a chat, after first checking whether he will charge for this. Some do; many do not. If you are eligible for legal aid you will have to go to a solicitor who deals with legal aid.

If you do not like the person you see, there is no obligation for you to continue, and conversely if he does not want to take you on for any reason, he can and will say so. On the whole a small firm will give you more time and understanding, and you are more likely to deal with a partner of that firm. A big firm will not only charge more, in all probability, but may well direct a junior or a clerk to deal with you.

LEGAL AID

You can obtain financial help with legal costs for fighting a divorce, including maintenance and custody; for contesting wills; for problems with housing, and so on.

There is no legal aid for undefended divorce proceedings, although if you are on supplementary benefit or family income supplement the court fee may be paid for you.

At the advice stage, you may qualify for free help or a reduced fee from a solicitor through two schemes. The Green Form Scheme means that a solicitor can give you up to £90 worth of advice free or at a reduced rate, with extensions if the case requires it. A Fixed Fee Interview means that for £5 you can get half-an-hour's advice. The Legal Aid Referral List (obtainable from Citizens' Advice Bureaux, libraries or the Law Society) will tell you which solicitors operate these schemes.

Legal aid is means-tested: you have to prove that your income is low enough to warrant aid. Both disposable income (income after tax, national insurance and allowances for dependents have been deducted) and disposable capital (savings, jewellery, etc., but not your house, furniture, fittings or clothes) are taken into account. Be prepared for your financial affairs to be thoroughly scrutinized.

Only a solicitor can apply for legal aid for you, and no specific figures are given here because so many variables affect the calculations. Your solicitor will help you with this.

If you are on supplementary benefit or family income supplement you will get legal aid without having to contribute anything. If you are within the legal limits but earning, you may have to make a contribution.

Remember that, for example, the sum of maintenance awarded to you will affect how much contribution you have to pay, as will any costs awarded to you. However, if you are receiving legal aid and you lose, you will not have to pay the other side's costs.

Before you decide to go to a solicitor you can visit a Citizens' Advice Bureau, one of the legal centres or a legal aid office for advice. The Law Society (address in Chapter 13) publishes two booklets, *Legal Aid Guide* and *Legal Aid – financial limits*, which may be of help. These can also be obtained from the places mentioned above.

FINDING A DOCTOR

If you are moving and want to find a local doctor, go and see your current doctor. He might be able to recommend someone else or help you find a doctor in the new neighbourhood. If you cannot or do not want to do that, the local chemist should be able to help and you will find a list of GPs practising in your area at your local post office, Citizens' Advice Bureau or public library. The Family Practitioner Committee (FPC) also has a list, and its number will be in the local telephone book under National Health Service, or in the London area under Family Practitioner Committee.

Go to see the practice you choose; if you do not feel happy about registering, for any reason, you are under no obligation to do so. The practice may not be able to take you on if its lists are full. This is sometimes the case in urban areas where the number of patients per doctor is very high.

If you change to a doctor in a different area, you must inform your old doctor and take or send your medical card to the surgery, having signed Part A. This will be forwarded to the FPC, which will register you, send you a new medical card and arrange for the transfer of your medical records.

If you are changing doctors but staying in the same area, your doctor has to sign a form giving his agreement to the change. If for some reason you do not want to see the doctor you can send your card to the FPC, which will attach a special form to the card allowing you to change without the signature of your present doctor. This can then be taken to your new doctor. If you have lost your medical card or do not have one, the FPC will get one for you.

Finding a private doctor is less easy. They are, as yet, not allowed to advertise, but friends, your own NHS doctor or the local chemist may be able to help. Your own NHS doctor may, of course, be willing to accept you as a private patient.

FINDING A DENTIST

You will also need a dentist. Do not forget that children receive free treatment until the age of sixteen, and if you are on supplementary benefit or family income supplement so will you.

Before joining a dentist's list, ask for recommendations from a friend, health visitor or doctor. The Family Practitioner Committee (FPC), listed in the local telephone directory under National Health Service or in London under Family Practitioner Committee, also has lists. If you are having any problems with your dentist (for example, he may not be prepared to carry out a particular treatment on the NHS), you can contact the FPC for advice.

It is normally easier to find a dentist than to find a doctor because the proportion of dentists per capita is higher.

FINDING OTHER SERVICES

If you have moved into a new area, or if you never had to deal with them before, finding good plumbers, builders, decorators and handymen can be tricky.

A friend who used to be in the building and decorating business used to say, 'It is only people who are lazy who have problems with builders, carpenters, decorators and plumbers. If you ring the first number you find, you can't be surprised if you get cowboys.' Recently he bought an old house to do up and the firm he hired, after a lot of research, turned out to be not only incompetent but extremely expensive.

The moral of this story is that when it comes to getting good workmen we are all in the same boat. Your best tactic is to ask around and use someone who is personally recommended.

Trade associations (see Chapter 13) can give you names of their members in your area, though not recommendations. The associations have codes of practice so the firms should therefore be reliable; at least you should have some comeback if things do go wrong.

Get more than one quote for the job in question, and make sure that you get the quotes in writing, that they specify exactly what is to be done, within what period of time, and detail the payment stages. The final payment should not be payable until the job has been finished to your satisfaction. Use your judgement, and do not automatically accept the cheapest quote. If you find it hard dealing with tradesmen or salesmen ask a friend in when they come round to discuss the job and prices. Someone who is not involved can often save you from making expensive mistakes.

If you have any complaints to make, first approach the firm concerned. If there is no response, go to the relevant trade association, if the firm is a member of one, and if not contact the Office of Fair Trading or a Citizens' Advice Bureau. CABs have a leaflet advising on how to protect yourself against unfair trading practices.

HOLIDAYS

Do not forget that you can get some very good bargain holidays if you are prepared to book at the last minute and do not mind where you go. Those on a limited budget may find this is the only way they can afford to go abroad.

Keep your passport up to date. You never know when you might suddenly get the chance to spend a weekend abroad. If your passport has run out you can get a temporary one, but it can be an effort – particularly if it has to be done at the last moment. If you do not have a passport, or you were on a family passport, apply for a new one (see page 137 for address or ask for a form at a post office).

If you have not had a passport before you will need photographic copies of your birth, marriage or divorce certificates. If you are applying for a separate passport, you will not need marriage or divorce certificates if you can provide the family passport.

If you have not been used to organizing tickets, time-tables and money for a trip abroad, make a list of everything you need well in advance, and keep referring to it. Give yourself plenty of time to check and double-check you have everything you need before you leave home. Ask the travel agent if you need any particular vaccinations. If you know someone who has been where you are going, ask about the place and try to glean some useful tips.

If you have to take any sort of medication make sure you have a good supply with you. It is better to take pills and lotions with you for every possible problem rather than try to find their foreign equivalents when a medical problem has arisen.

Unless you want to invite burglars into your home, remember to cancel the papers and milk, and ask someone to check that letters and circulars are not left sticking out of the letter-box while you are away. Tell the neighbours where you are going, and for how long. If possible give them a telephone number where you can be reached. It is also worth letting the local police station know.

For ideas about holidays specifically for single people, see Chapter 9.

CHAPTER 12

Money

Now you are on your own you will need to give your financial position some serious thought, especially if you have not been used to dealing with money matters. You will want to use your assets to the best advantage, particularly if you have only a small income.

Whether professional advice is desirable or necessary will depend on the size and nature of your income and capital. If you have only a small amount of capital you do not necessarily need an accountant to advise you where to invest: your bank manager will be able to help. If your financial affairs are straightforward you can complete your own tax return. Any tax office will help you fill in a tax return, or any other forms the Inland Revenue may require you to complete. (The Bibliography lists specialist books on tax and money.)

On the other hand, if you have a substantial amount of money to invest or you need specialized help with your tax, you should find a reputable accountant. Good advice will cost money, but an accountant's fees can be saved several times over by his expertise; even the peace of mind brought by knowing your affairs are being taken care of could be worth the expense.

FINDING AN ACCOUNTANT

It is very important that you like and trust the accountant you use, especially if you know little or nothing about tax or investing money.

If you are a widow you might wish to go to your husband's accountant, if he had one. If you are separated or divorced you can still use the same accountant as your partner, but you might not wish to do so. Talk to as many people as possible; find out who looks after their tax and money affairs and whom they trust and respect from their own experience. If this does not lead to an introduction, you could ask your bank manager (although he is likely to recommend a bank customer). If you cannot get a personal recommendation, the Citizens' Advice Bureau or Institute of Chartered Accountants (address in Chapter 13) will give you lists of reputable accountancy firms in your area; or you could try looking in the *Yellow Pages* of the telephone directory.

Country accountants may charge less than city accountants, because they often have a smaller practice and lower overheads. Usually one pays proportionately more for larger firms.

When you see an accountant, explain your exact position and what advice and help you need. Ask him what his hourly rates are and whether he can give you some idea of how long he might need to deal with your affairs. Although this is often difficult to do he should have some idea and be able to give you an estimate of the cost. Check with friends to see how much their accountants charge them. If you feel the accountant you have just seen is too expensive, unsympathetic, or does not understand your needs, go and see another one.

When you have chosen an accountant ask him what information he needs from you. If you can supply comprehensive and organized paperwork his work will be less. Try not to bother him with problems you can resolve yourself, because this will cost you money.

WHERE TO INVEST

There is no universal answer to this, as so much depends on individual circumstances. Suffice it to say that one needs quite a lot of money to justify 'dabbling' on the stock market. If you have less than £30,000 free capital, invest in things which are safe and simple. If you have more than that you need an adviser who understands investments. Here are a few guidelines.

Bank accounts

If you have surplus to your everyday needs in your current account, but that amount is not large enough to warrant investing elsewhere, you should put it in a deposit account and let it accrue interest. It is always advisable to have a lump sum of money which is readily available in case of emergencies, and there is no restriction in withdrawing money (except that you may lose seven days' interest) from deposit accounts.

Banks also have various savings accounts which earn different rates of interest – as much as three per cent above normal deposit account interest – according to the withdrawal restrictions, how much and how often the money is paid in, and so on.

Building society deposits
Choose the society which seems best able to look after your particular needs. The account with the highest rate of interest may not necessarily be the best if you think you may need to withdraw money quickly or if it has very stringent conditions for mortgages, for example. Check on the notice required for withdrawals of cash, and remember that building societies are open for longer hours than banks, as well as on Saturdays, which can be useful.

Tax on bank and building society deposits
The interest you earn on bank and building society deposits is taxed at source at the basic rate. Whereas for other types of income on which non-taxpayers can claim back the tax removed at source, this tax is not refundable. So if you are not a taxpayer it is not a good idea to put your money into building societies or bank deposit accounts.

National Savings Income Bonds
If you want a source of monthly income it would be worth looking at these. Bonds can be bought at post offices and the interest can be paid into your bank account. This is taxable income, but as the interest is paid in full (before tax is deducted) it is attractive to anyone not subject to income tax. Withdrawal terms are more restrictive than for most investments, so you should check these before investing.

Annuities
If you are over 70 and are prepared to dispense with capital to buy an annuity, this is worth while because a good part of the income is tax-free. It depends on your age how much is tax-free, and it is advisable to ask an insurance broker or your accountant about the best one to get, especially as some annuities repay part of the capital in certain circumstances on one's death.

Government stocks

If you like the security of government stocks, unless you are a high taxpayer go for those which give a high return. The actual cost of these alters daily (depending on the financial market), but the interest for each issue is fixed, which can be an advantage if you buy stock when interest rates are high. You can sell them at any time, or keep them until the specified redemption date. Some stocks can be bought at post offices and interest on these is paid in full without tax being deducted at source (as it is if you buy stocks through a broker). You can get advice on buying stocks from your bank or accountant.

Income bonds

Regularly advertised in the press, these are high-income guaranteed bonds, but because they are so complicated it is a good idea to take professional advice before investing in them.

National Savings Certificates

These are usually attractive to higher-rate taxpayers. They have to be kept for a full five years to achieve maximum benefit, so are suitable only for people who do not need immediate income from their capital.

INLAND REVENUE

If you have become a widow or widower you should inform the tax office of your spouse's death as soon as possible in order to get his or her tax affairs sorted out and to find out whether any tax refund is due, unless this is being done by a solicitor or accountant.

If you do not know which office to inform, look for any letters from the tax office to the deceased – the address and personal reference number will be there; or ask the deceased's employer for his or her PAYE tax district and reference number.

If you are paying tax and have become single for any reason you must inform your own tax office, because your tax code may need to be changed and the allowances due to you as a single person will be different if you were previously taxed as part of a married couple. Your allowance may increase if you are over 65, depending on your income. Every single parent with a child, including a stepchild or an adopted child under the age of 18, gets an extra allowance. To qualify, the child must live with the parent who claims the allowance and be under 16; if the child is over 16, he must either be in full-time education or be receiving full-time training by an employer for not less than two years.

Widows
The widow's allowance is the same as a single person's allowance. If you are over 65 and your income is below a certain level you can also claim the age allowance. If your husband was receiving the married man's allowance you will be able to claim a widow's bereavement allowance – which is the same as the married man's allowance – for the rest of the tax year after his death and for the following year.

If you are receiving widow's benefit, widow's pension or widowed mother's allowance from the Department of Health and Social Security (DHSS) you will have to pay tax on these. You do not pay tax on extra benefits for children. A widower does not at present receive benefits for himself, except that he will continue to receive the married man's allowance for the rest of the tax year in which his wife died, and he can apply for the additional personal allowance if he has dependent children.

Divorcees or separated partners
From the time you separate, that is, are living apart from your partner permanently, your tax situation changes.

A woman who was taxed jointly with her husband will now be taxed as a single person. If you are looking after a child you should receive the additional personal allowance, which will bring your allowance up to the same level as a married man's allowance.

A man who has been receiving the married man's allowance is entitled to claim it for the whole of the first tax year after his separation; or until the divorce is absolute if he is paying voluntary maintenance to his wife upon which she is entirely dependent (that is, she is receiving no other form of income). After that he will be taxed as a single man.

MAINTENANCE PAYMENTS
Small maintenance payments (see Chapter 14) payable under a court order are paid in full with no tax taken off.

The payer can then claim these payments against any other tax he is paying. The recipient will, however, have to pay tax on the payments unless her income is below the tax threshold.

Larger maintenance payments or regular payments under a deed or legal agreement are paid after tax has been deducted. The payer can get tax relief, and the recipient – if she has not used up her tax allowance, or does not pay tax at all – can claim the deducted tax. This enables both parties to get as much benefit from the payments as possible.

Maintenance payments for children can be paid directly to them, instead of to the mother or father looking after them. This can be advantageous because children have their own tax allowances and therefore can 'earn' a certain amount before paying tax. For example, if maintenance is £3000 and it is all paid to you, you will have to pay tax on anything over your allowance. If you have two children and this sum is paid to the three of you, no tax will have to be paid because each amount is below the single person's allowance.

On the other hand, maintenance will normally end when the children reach 16 or when they have completed their full-time education, and you may prefer to have everything consolidated into one payment for yourself from the start. It is worth getting advice on this. Your accountant or laywer, or the National Association for One-Parent Families (details in Chapter 13) will help you work out the best arrangement.

Do not forget that if you are paying a mortgage you will receive tax relief on the interest. It can, in fact, often be advantageous for the custodial parent to take over the mortgage and get increased maintenance to cover the mortgage payments. This will also leave the partner free to claim tax relief on his own mortgage if he owns a property separately.

If you are a middle-aged wife, it is worth considering, when you are working out the divorce settlement, the loss of national insurance and pension benefits you would have received as a widow. The pension often includes a lump sum already nominated to the wife in the event of the death of her husband before retirement age.

If your ex-husband re-marries he can nominate this sum to be paid to his new wife, but if he is happy to leave it to be paid to you it is important for this to be stated in the divorce settlement. If your ex-husband re-marries, you will not benefit on his death from any of his occupational pensions, although you will receive a full state pension as long as you started paying national insurance contributions after the divorce. It is a good idea to think about how you will be provided for in your old age, as well as at present.

BENEFITS FROM THE DHSS

Widow's allowance
If you are a widow you are entitled to your husband's pension, but a widower is not entitled to his wife's pension if she was due one. However, he can use his wife's contribution record to make up his own basic pension.

For the first 26 weeks you will receive a widow's allowance if you were under 60 when your husband died and he was paying full contributions. If you were over 60 you will receive a widow's pension which takes account of both your husband's and your own contributions.

After 26 weeks you will receive a widowed mother's allowance if you have a child under 19 living with you; or a widow's pension if you were over 40 when your husband died and you do not receive a widowed mother's allowance. If you have no children living with you and are under 40 you will receive no further benefits.

If you are over 60 you will receive a full pension. Between the ages of 40 and 60 this is reduced, increasing yearly until the full amount is reached.

If you go back to work you do not lose your allowances as such; however, all pensions can be affected by earnings (unless you are a man over 70 or a woman over 65, when other earnings make no difference).

If you are a divorced mother who has not re-married and your ex-husband, who has been paying maintenance to support your child, dies, you can claim the child's special allowance. You should claim this as soon as possible: it is worth more than one-parent benefit, but you cannot claim both.

Supplementary benefit
If you are widowed and your husband did not pay his contributions, or you are separated or divorced and short of

money, you can claim supplementary benefit for yourself and any children living with you under 16 (or up to 19 if in full-time education) if you work less than 24 hours a week, or family income supplement if you work more than 24 hours a week.

To claim supplementary benefit you have to have less than £3000 in savings or investments. If you start working this will affect your supplementary benefit, depending on how much you earn. As a single parent you do not have to sign on to get supplementary benefit, and you can earn more than if you were still married before it affects the benefit you receive. (See Chapter 11.)

If you are receiving supplementary benefit you will also get help towards heating costs and you can ask for a lump sum for such items as removal costs, special clothing, and so on. You can also claim legal aid if you are fighting a divorce case, custody or maintenance. (See Chapter 14.)

After being on supplementary benefit for a year you can claim a higher long-term rate. You receive child benefit in the normal way, and you can also claim one-parent benefit.

One-parent benefit

When you separate you should apply for one-parent benefit after 13 weeks of separation; if divorced or legally separated you should claim straight away. If you start living with someone as a husband or wife you cannot then claim one-parent benefit, nor widow's benefit.

Family income supplement

If you work full-time (more than 24 hours a week), but earn under the prescribed amount you can claim family income supplement (FIS). FIS is paid for 52 weeks and if your earnings change during that period the amount you receive will not be altered. You must re-apply at the end of the year.

Those on family income supplement and supplementary benefit can claim free prescriptions; free NHS dental treatment and glasses; free milk and vitamins for any children under school-age, and for pregnant women; refunds of fares to and from hospital for treatment; and free school meals.

Unemployment, statutory sick pay and sickness benefits

If you are receiving a widow's allowance you will not get

unemployment or sickness benefit, unless it is worth more than the widow's allowance, because you cannot claim two at once. If you are paying reduced national insurance contributions because you are a widow you will not qualify for unemployment or sickness benefit. You can, however, claim statutory sick pay (which you get from your employer, rather than from the DHSS) as this does not rely on national insurance payments, and you can claim this on top of your widow's benefit.

Housing benefits
You can claim help with your rent, rates and mortgage interest repayments if you have a low income. The rebates can be very complicated to work out, and will depend on what your essential outgoings are, how much you earn, and what dependents you have. The DHSS works out your 'needs allowance', and the rebates are set against this.

If you are on supplementary benefit you automatically qualify for certificated housing benefits. This means you will not have to pay rent or rates if you are living in council property; if in other accommodation, you will be given money to cover or help with the rent and rates. If you are not getting supplementary benefit you can claim for standard housing benefit, which helps with rates or rent; and even if you are earning quite a high salary, but you have high outgoings, you might qualify for this.

If you just fail to qualify for supplementary benefit, you can also apply for housing benefit supplement, which is in addition to the standard housing benefit. This will also entitle you to free glasses, prescriptions and dental treatment.

NATIONAL INSURANCE PAYMENTS
If you are working and you were paying the married woman's reduced national insurance payment directly before you were widowed you may continue to do so, as long as your husband paid his full contributions; this means you will receive a pension based on his contributions as well as your own. If you think you will ever remarry or cohabit, you should start paying the full amount immediately, because by remarrying or cohabiting you will lose the right to benefit from your husband's contributions.

If you are separated or divorced you will have to pay the

full national insurance contribution unless you are receiving child benefit payments; if you are looking after a child under sixteen and you promise to pay the full contribution ('stamp') when you start working again, you do not have to pay the full contribution in the interim. Thanks to Home Responsibilities Protection, your right to a basic pension is protected while you stay at home to look after children. In this case your payments will be credited. It is essential you go to your local DHSS office to find out what you should be paying – and, indeed, what your entitlements are.

If you are uncertain whether you are receiving the correct benefits, or unsure about what national insurance you should be paying contact a Citizens' Advice Bureau, Cruse (the National Organization for the Widowed), the Family Welfare Association, the National Council for One-Parent Families or the Child Poverty Action Group. (See Chapter 13.)

INSURANCE

It is most important that your insurance is kept up to date, and you are fully covered. If the insurance of your home and car was always looked after by your spouse, it is easy to forget all about it now you are on your own.

Phyllis, an elderly widow living in the country, fell into the common trap of assuming that just because she had kept up insurance payments she was adequately insured: 'I didn't realize until I was burgled that, to my horror, although I had paid my insurance premium regularly, I was grossly under-insured. The last time the policy had been looked at was 15 years ago before my husband died. It had never occurred to me to update it because of inflation.'

If you need a new policy it is sensible to go to an insurance broker, who will know which are the best policies on the market and which one will best suit your needs. If you cannot get a recommendation from a friend, bank or accountant, ask the Insurance Brokers' Association to give you a list of reputable brokers in your area (see Chapter 13). Otherwise, the Citizens' Advice Bureau could advise you.

Remember to check items such as car tax and parking permits. It is easy, when you have not been in the habit of dealing with them, to let annual payments fall behind.

Make sure that if you buy new things for the house – an armchair, a freezer, a new bed – these are included on your insurance. Watch out for the small print that specifies, for instance, that jewellery has to be listed separately. A good broker should point this out to you, but it is very easy to assume that everything is covered under 'general contents' only to find out, when it is too late, that some items should have been listed separately and you can claim only a small percentage of the total value.

Another very important safeguard to consider is a personal insurance policy. If you have children it is a good idea to have life assurance. If you are self-employed you should have a policy covering illness or accident which might stop you being able to earn. A small savings policy which matures when you are older can be very worthwhile. There are thousands of different policies on the market and you must get advice from an expert. Be careful about policies from door-to-door salesmen, or from glossy advertisements in papers and magazines. A *good* scheme is rarely sold by such means: but there could be exceptions, so consult your broker.

FINDING A BANK

If you are unlucky enough to have a bank manager with whom you cannot communicate, or who is unsympathetic, change your bank immediately. It is not as difficult to do as you might think. Make appointments to see the managers of several different local banks. Tell them exactly what your situation is: whether you need help budgeting your money, whether you need a loan, or whatever. The one you feel happiest with will be the best person to help you sort out your finances.

OBTAINING A LOAN

You may need to borrow money – to tide you over while probate is being sorted out, perhaps, or because you need a new cooker, refrigerator or car; or perhaps you want a mortgage.

For a short-term loan your bank manager would be the best person to approach. You can either get a personal loan which you pay back at a fixed rate per month, or an overdraft, which is the cheapest way to borrow small amounts of money.

You could ask a friend or relation to lend you the money, but if you do it would be wise – however well you know or get on with the individual concerned – to do it in a business-like manner. Although you need not use a solicitor, it is a good idea to write down all the details of the loan with the terms of repayment clearly set out and signed by both parties. If anything should happen to either of you, the other then has proof of the loan and matters can proceed from there. And if any argument between the two of you should arise, you will be able to prove the terms agreed and if need be get them backed by law.

You can apply for a mortgage from a building society, bank, housing association or local authority. Find out which interest rates are lowest and, more importantly, which mortgage is best for your needs. Do not ignore the special deals now being offered such as free surveys, free life assurance and so on. They could save you money. Repayments often include insurance cover on the mortgage; but if they do not you must insure the mortgage, to protect yourself and your children if anything should happen to you.

Finance companies also lend money, but usually at a very high interest rate. Make sure you read the small print before entering into any agreement, and check exactly what the annual interest rate is.

Hire purchase is also an expensive way to borrow money. If you are working you may be able to service your HP debts: but what if you are suddenly made redundant? You may do better to buy major items with a bank credit card so that you can spread the payment: if you are able to pay off the amount spent within the month of billing you will not need to pay interest on it.

PROBATE

If your partner dies, you will need to sort out probate as a matter of some urgency. If the estate is very small, it is mostly unnecessary to obtain a grant of probate: for example, a small estate might comprise some cash, a car and some furniture. If the assets are held by bodies such as the Department of National Savings, building societies and so on, you usually need do no more than write to the relevant body explaining the circumstances. You will be sent the appropriate form, which must be completed and returned with the correct death certificate.

Usually a solicitor will deal with probate, but if you think the estate is straightforward you can apply for probate yourself. Solicitors' fees vary from firm to firm, and also depend on the size of the estate. However, they usually charge between 1 and 3 per cent of the probate granted, so it is well worth asking more than one solicitor what he will charge.

If you want to do without a solicitor, either the executor of the will or next-of-kin may apply for probate within two weeks of the death. You will find addresses of probate offices in the telephone directory; or you could ask a solicitor, or, alternatively, write to the personal application department of the Probate Registry. (See Chapter 13.)

If you obtain probate by private application you will have to pay probate registry fees, which are based on a sliding scale, a court fee and a departmental fee.

The time probate takes to be granted does not depend just on the amount of money involved. The estate might be small but it might, for example, be invested in such a way to make its release very difficult. On the other hand the deceased may have had his money in one building society share account from which it can be easily extracted.

If you are cut out of your partner's will in England or Wales you may challenge it: go and see a solicitor. If you have little money yourself you could apply for legal aid. (See Chapter 11.) In Scotland, however, the wife and children always have a right to part of the estate – one-third to the wife and one-third to the children; it is illegal to cut them out completely.

If the deceased died intestate (i.e. he or she did not make a will) the estate will be divided according to law. This differs according to the law of the country: Scotland has different rules from England and your solicitor will advise you on this.

It is in everyone's interest to make a will.

Everything that your partner owned – the house, money, life assurances, jewellery, personal possessions and so on – has to be valued, and if the amount exceeds a specified figure you will have to pay capital transfer tax. (See Chapter 14.)

The probate forms look, and are, quite complicated and must be filled in precisely and correctly. If you are doing them yourself the personal application department has staff on hand to help you; otherwise you could get help from your accountant, bank manager or someone else with experience of probate.

It is worth noting that if the estate is a simple one and you want the matter dealt with quickly, it might be worth applying to a sub-probate registry. These are the small offices outside major cities. You do not have to live in the area where the registry is, and because they are on the whole less busy, matters are dealt with more quickly. However, the disadvantage of getting the probate dealt with in a sub-probate registry is that you usually have to see the probate officer at least twice in person.

An estate that is complicated – tied up in trusts, companies, and so on – can take several years to be sorted out and you will have to wait patiently until you know exactly how much you will receive. Solicitors will not ask for their full bill to be paid until probate has been granted, but they will ask for some monies on account.

While you are waiting for probate to be proved any money in your spouse's account will be frozen, but if you desperately need cash, your bank manager will help you. Banks cannot let money out of a frozen account, but they can set up a separate overdraft or loan account for you.

If your bank account was a joint one the account will stay open, but a word of warning: some people find it upsetting when, after seeing the death certificate, the bank removes their partner's name from the account.

CHAPTER 13

Where to go for help

This chapter covers associations, clubs, companies and organizations which can help in circumstances of bereavement, separation or divorce. It also includes names and addresses which relate to information in the main text, information concerning the conciliation and counselling services and practical help sources

Chapter 2 BEREAVEMENT
Documents
The following should be returned to their issuing offices:
(1) Passport: unless it was a family passport and you wish to apply for a separate one (in which case you will need it), send the deceased's passport to the relevant Passport Office, depending on which area you live in: Clive House, 70 Petty France, London SW1H 9HD; Empire House, 131 West Nile Street, Glasgow G1 2RY; India Buildings, Water Street, Liverpool L2 0QZ; Olympia House, Upper Dock Street, Newport, Gwent NPT 1XA; 55 Westfield Road, Peterborough PE3 6TG; Hampton House, 47–53 High Street, Belfast BT1 2QS.
(2) Driving licence and logbook to DVLC, Swansea SA6 7GL.
(3) Medical card to the Family Practitioner Committee, whose address is in the local telephone directory under National Health Service or, in the London area, under Family Practitioner Committee.

Organizations
CRUSE (National Organization for the Widowed and their Children), Cruse House, 126 Sheen Road, Richmond, Surrey TW9 1UR. Tel: 01-940 4818.
Cruse offers a counselling service for widows and widowers. It has 100 branches and will advise on any matter including social, welfare, financial and legal problems.

Cruse holds gatherings all over Britain for people needing to talk to others in the same situation, or who just want to exchange views and feelings. Though more of a staging post at a difficult time than a long-term source of support, it also runs social clubs for elderly widowed people.

NATIONAL ASSOCIATION OF WIDOWS, Voluntary Service Centre, Chell Road, Stafford ST16 2QA. Tel: 0785 45465.

There are 74 branches all over the country, offering advice and support; information on legal and financial matters; how and what to claim from the DHSS; education, training and retraining. Members of the association can give comfort and discuss problems from the standpoint of their own experience and understanding.

Through its branches the association provides a social life for widows and widowers, and a point of contact for people who feel they cannot face their own friends for a time. It also organizes outings and visits to other branches. Membership is free.

MOTHERS' UNION, Mary Sumner House, 24 Tufton Street, London SW1 3RB. Tel: 01-222 5533.

The Social Concern department of the Mothers' Union has members trained in bereavement counselling. They can also give practical support by looking after children, helping with babysitting rotas and advising on problems in the home. There are branches all over Great Britain, with 'listening posts' in certain areas where trained counsellors offer help to anyone needing to talk or wanting advice.

The Union also has holiday schemes: guesthouse and caravan holidays; hostess holidays; and holidays for needy families.

Chapter 3 SEPARATION AND DIVORCE

NATIONAL FAMILY CONCILIATION COUNCIL, Romany Cottage, Crawley, Winchester, Hampshire SO21 2PR.

There are 22 affiliated conciliation councils and thirty more in the process of being formed. If you get in touch with the National Council you will be sent the address of your nearest one. The Council offers a neutral third party to help resolve difficulties and provide a completely confidential service. If you are dealing with solicitors it will liaise with them, with your permission. It is currently trying to integrate out-of-court counselling with in-court mediation.

For a one-hour interview you will be asked for a donation, usually about £7. If you are receiving legal aid the council's fee may be reclaimed through the Law Society.

DIVORCE, CONCILIATION AND ADVISORY SERVICE, 38 Ebury Street, London SW1 0LU. Tel: 01-730 2422.
This small advisory service deals with counselling and conciliation, especially in regard to access and custody. Many of its clients contact the service when they are thinking about separation and want to find out what life will be like on their own; it also advises on loneliness and re-building a social life.

The fee for the first interview is £15 and the following ones are negotiable, charges ranging from £5 to £10. If you are receiving social security benefit, there is no charge.

For conciliation each partner is first seen separately, at a charge of £15 each, then together, which costs £20. If you are receiving legal aid your solicitor will pay £30, which he can claim back from the Law Society.

BRITISH ASSOCIATION OF COUNSELLING, 37a Sheeps Street, Rugby CV21 3BX. Tel: 0788 78328.
This acts as an information service for anyone who needs counselling. It will recommend relevant associations or its own individual local counsellors, who are spread throughout Britain.

NATIONAL MARRIAGE GUIDANCE COUNCIL, Herbert Gray College, Little Church Street, Rugby, Warwickshire CV21 3AP. Tel: 0788 73241.
There are 150 branches in England, Wales and Northern Ireland (listed in the telephone directory). Marriage guidance councils exist not only to reconcile marriage partnerships in trouble. They will see anybody, heterosexual or homosexual, who needs help, including those going through a separation or divorce or having difficulties after being divorced.

There is a waiting-list for appointments at some branches,

but a reception interview scheme operates for which the waiting-time is much shorter. At these interviews staff ascertain what sort of help you need, maybe recommending you to another source of help such as a solicitor, or giving you an appointment to see one of their advisers.

Fees are about £8 for one session, depending on the means of the individual.

SCOTTISH MARRIAGE GUIDANCE COUNCIL, 26 Frederick Street, Edinburgh EH2 2JR. Tel: 031 225 5006.
There are 18 local councils, with 50 counselling centres and 160 counsellors, throughout Scotland.

CATHOLIC MARRIAGE GUIDANCE COUNCIL, 15 Lansdowne Road, London W11 3AJ. Tel: 01-727 0141.
There are 80 branches throughout Britain and you will be referred to your nearest branch. Branches are advertised in most churches, libraries and relevant publications. The Council will advise and help anyone going through separation or divorce, and will see single parents with their children, especially if there are teenage problems. There is no fee, but you are expected to make a donation in accordance with your financial position.

JEWISH MARRIAGE GUIDANCE COUNCIL, 23 Ravenshurst Avenue, London NW4 4EL. Tel: 01-203 6311.
The Council offers advice to those experiencing problems with their personal relationships, whether separated, divorced, widowed, or planning to re-marry; it also runs a friendship bureau with branches in London and Manchester. There is no charge for counselling, but a voluntary contribution, according to means, is requested towards expenses.

WESTMINSTER PASTORAL FOUNDATION, 23 Kensington Square, London W8 5HN. Tel: 01-937 6956.
The Foundation, with 28 centres throughout Britain and a highly trained staff, offers help to anyone needing to talk about emotional problems. Although it is not a religious organization it is concerned with spiritual values.

You must be prepared to talk freely, because the Foundation will wish to discuss your life as a whole: your past; your feelings towards your parents and your siblings; your emotional experiences.

You can be seen one to one; in groups of six to eight people with a group leader; or you can attend with your children. The Foundation will also help with children's problems.

Payment for counselling is by voluntary contribution according to means (negotiation of the fee forms part and parcel of the counselling).

NATIONAL COUNCIL FOR THE DIVORCED AND SEPARATED, 13 High Street, Little Shelford, Cambridge CB2 5ES.

There are over 130 branches in Britain and new branches are continually being started. Formed to provide a venue where people with similar experiences and problems can meet in a relaxed and sympathetic atmosphere, the Council has experienced welfare officers who will advise on, for example, financial, emotional or social difficulties. Or you can just talk to other members who are in the same situation as you. The Council offers a good way to make new friends, build a new social life and receive help from sympathetic people. The general aim is to lift people back into society and to give them confidence. Each branch organizes social functions, coffee mornings, outings and holidays, for adults alone or with their children. Membership costs about £2.50 a year, covering access to all branches, and a small fee is charged for social events. Before you can join, you must satisfy the Council that you are separated or divorced.

ASSOCIATION OF SEPARATED AND DIVORCED CATHOLICS, The Holy Name Presbytery, 8 Portsmouth Street, Manchester M13 9GB. Tel: 061 969 0741 or 061 865 1504.

This association, run by volunteers, has 40 branches throughout Britain.

Each branch operates slightly differently, depending on the particular needs of the area, but in general they can provide legal, financial and welfare advice, they organize socials and outings and they provide a contact point for single Catholics in the area. Officers can often only be contacted in the evenings, and it is better to write for the address and telephone number of your nearest branch.

BROKEN RITES, 44 Vandon Court, Petty France, London SW1H 9HF. Tel: 01-222 7291, evenings only.
This is an independent, inter-denominational support group set up to help when a member of the clergy's marriage breaks down. It provides practical assistance, such as lists of temporary and permanent accommodation; advice on rights and legal problems (it can provide names of lawyers who are members of the Lawyers' Christian Fellowship); and sympathetic listeners, especially important in the case of breakdowns within clergy marriages because of the frequent need for secrecy.

WOMEN'S AID FEDERATION, 52/54 Featherstone Street, London EC1. Tel: 01-251 6537.
The Women's Aid Federation, with 30 branches in London and other branches throughout Britain, is for women at risk: battered women, or any woman who is in home circumstances that are detrimental to her physical or mental health. If you are in this position, and are contemplating leaving your husband, these are the people to contact. They will take you in, help you with re-housing, or get you back to your home when it has been vacated. If you have no money they will immediately contact the social services on your behalf, or help you themselves if necessary. They have accommodation for both women and children at various refuges, the addresses of which are known only to the Federation, which will also refer you to the other associations if necessary.

If you cannot find the number of your nearest branch the social services, Citizens' Advice Bureau or the national office at the above number will help.

CHILD POVERTY ACTION GROUP, 1 Macklin Street, London WC2B 5NH. Tel: 01-242 3225.
There are 35 branches, covering most of Britain; addresses can be obtained from the above office.
As well as campaigning against child poverty, the Group provides practical assistance to any family that is having money problems. It will help you to claim the benefits to which you are entitled, and to fight if you think you are not getting what you should. It also publishes self-help guides

and runs a free information, advisory and advocacy service.

FAMILY WELFARE ASSOCIATION, 501/505 Kingsland Road, Dalston, London E8 4AU. Tel: 01-254 6251.
Though independent, this association, with 10 London offices and others in Northampton and Milton Keynes, works closely with the social services in many cases. It will help with emotional and practical problems, and will refer you to other associations if necessary.

You can either attend for a private interview, or someone will come to your home, if you prefer. All services are free. The association has a 'Drop In' shop at 608 Holloway Road, London N19 (Tel: 01-272 1551) where you can have a cup of coffee, chat about your problems and ask advice as well as buy items for the family. Besides the conciliation service based at 313 Shrewsbury Road, London E7, tel: 01-470 3939 (open from 9.30 am to 5.30 pm), each branch has its own conciliation service that will, for example, help you sort out a divorce in the most amenable way, including access for children.

For numbers of branches, ring the central office.

SALVATION ARMY, Central Office, 101 Queen Victoria Street, London EC4. Tel: 01-236 7020.
The Salvation Army has 1000 branches, which welcome all those, regardless of religious beliefs, who wish to talk about their problems; there are no strings attached.

The Army will help you sort out straightforward problems such as filling in forms or dealing with complicated bills, or will, if necessary, refer you to a professional counsellor. In many areas the Army's social service centres or hostels are open seven days a week, and you can just turn up for a chat or advice.

In London there is a specific counselling centre at 177 Whitechapel Road, London E1 1DP (tel: 01-247 0669) which helps with emotional problems. The offices are open for telephone calls from 9.00 am to 4.30 pm on weekdays, but counselling often takes place in the evenings as well.

SAMARITANS
There are 180 branches throughout Britain, open 24 hours a day, and if you cannot find the number in the telephone

book the operator will put you through. Founded in 1953, the Samaritans offer a free and completely confidential befriending service to anyone who needs it – the depressed, the worried and the suicidal. Most local branches are open to visitors in the daytime and evenings. Or you can communicate by letter: three branches deal specifically with correspondence: P.O. Box B8, Huddersfield HD1 1HR; P.O. Box 10, Northallerton, N. Yorkshire DL7 8XW; P.O. Box 9, Sterling, Scotland FK8 2SA.

BROOK ADVISORY CENTRES, Central Office, 153a East Street, London SE17 2SD. Tel: 01-708 1234.
The first centre was opened in 1964 and there are now 16 spread throughout Britain (London, Edinburgh, Birmingham, Coventry, Merseyside and Bristol). They are financed by the National Health Service and although the emphasis is on educating young people about sex, they will counsel people of any age with sex-related problems that are affecting a relationship, whether leading to the break-up of a partnership or causing problems after a break-up.
Most of their services are free.

NATIONAL COUNCIL FOR ONE-PARENT FAMILIES, 255 Kentish Town Road, London NW5 2LX. Tel: 01-267 1361.
This council works to improve the position of lone parents and their children; its aim is to secure financial, legal and social equality for one-parent families.
If you live in a London borough south of the Thames, contact One-Parent Families, South London Advice Centre, 20 Clapham Common South Side, London SW4 7AB, tel: 01-720 9191. Otherwise, contact the above office.
The Council's welfare officers will advise on tax, accommodation, finance and legal problems, and will in fact help with most situations facing a single parent with children. They can recommend lawyers; suggest sources of specialist advice; advise on applying for legal aid; and give details of social clubs, networks and associations. They can sort out social security payments and help you to decide, for instance, whether it is more advantageous to work or take supplementary benefit. The Council produces many useful leaflets for one-parent families.

SCOTTISH COUNCIL FOR SINGLE PARENTS, 13 Gayfield Square, Edinburgh EH1 3NX. Tel: 031 556 3899.
This council works on the same principles as the National Council for One-Parent Families (see above).

FAMILIES NEED FATHERS, 59 Schubert Road, London SW15. (Ansaphone where you can leave your name and address for information: 01-852 7123.)
Families Need Fathers was set up in 1974 to help noncustodial parents, and although these are usually fathers a good proportion of mothers are also members. There are groups in London, Bristol, Birmingham, Scotland, South Wales, Kent and the North East. Membership costs £10 for the first year, and £8 per annum thereafter.

The organization will advise on problems, give you a chance to talk to other people in similar situations, and produces a comprehensive booklet on the rights of noncustodial parents. There is also a newsletter for members. Regular 'Walk-In Talk-In' sessions are held on the first and third Fridays of each month from 7.30 to 9.30 pm at Conway Hall, Red Lion Square, London WC1, at which all (including non-members) are welcome.

The association strives for fairer treatment of both parents in divorce cases, maintaining, to the child's best advantage, that parents have equal rights as well as equal responsibilities and that the child's relationship with both parents must be preserved in the event of a marital break-up.

MOTHERS' UNION (Social Concern) can also help separated or divorced people (see page 138).

Chapter 4 LONELINESS

GINGERBREAD, 35 Wellington Street, London WC2 7BN. Tel: 01-240 0953.
Gingerbread is an association of one-parent families, with a network of over 300 self-help groups throughout Britain, and has approximately 13,000 members. Each group, run entirely by single parents, differs in size and scope of activity. The aims of Gingerbread are to provide meeting-places for parents and children, information and advice, practical help in bringing up children, and moral and

emotional support from people who are going through, or have gone through, a marital break-up.

A Gingerbread group can help with babysitting, for example, by organizing rotas. (One group in London hired a room from a youth group every Saturday evening from 8.00 to 11.00 pm; mothers took it in turns to look after the children of those in their group. With this system each mother had the companionship of another adult while looking after the children, as well as getting out of her own home for an evening.) Gingerbread also organizes holidays for both parents and children.

Some groups are comprised solely of women, some only of men; many are mixed. Those who find solace and friendship within these groups when first alone may later move on to other organizations if they wish to find a 'mate'.

SINGLEHANDED LTD, Thorne House, Hankham Place, Stone Cross, Pevensey, East Sussex BN24 5ER. Tel: 0323 767507.

This is a nationwide organization that helps with accommodation, holidays and babysitting, and provides both counselling and practical advice. It puts single parents in touch with each other so that they can share homes, and thus halve the costs, and can help single-handed fathers find a single woman (with or without children) to act as substitute mother in return for accommodation, full board and allowance.

The company also has a friendship and contact service, and organizes holidays, in Britain and abroad, including short breaks and holidays for children only.

Annual membership costs £30.

CITIZENS' ADVICE BUREAUX

There are over 900 of these, one in every major town in Great Britain, with reference files, addresses and telephone numbers relating to practically any problem or query that can arise: housing, legal or financial problems, social security, family welfare; how to find a doctor, or an accountant, and so on. They will also act as an intermediary and help you write letters or fill in forms.

They are the only general advice service, and if they do not know the answer to your query they will refer you to the right people.

Some bureaux, particularly those in inner city areas, are busier than others, and you may find they do not have much time to spare for each individual, so it may be wise to ring first for an appointment. Outside major cities you can just walk in, or phone.

The bureaux have leaflets on most of the subjects they cover.

The address of your local Citizens' Advice Bureau will be in the telephone directory; otherwise, ask at a library or post office.

Chapter 5 HEALTH

RELAXATION FOR LIVING, Dunesk, 29 Burwood Park Road, Walton-upon-Thames, Surrey KT12 5LH.
This organization, now with teachers throughout Britain, was set up ten years ago to teach people how to deal with stress, how to relax and how to enjoy relaxing. Teachers work either from their own homes, in town halls or at local health clinics. Write to them for a newsletter containing articles, information and book reviews, and details of all classes and meetings. Annual membership is £3.00.

BRITISH WHEEL OF YOGA, 80 Lechampton Road, Cheltenham, Gloucester.
This, the main yoga association in the UK, has qualified teachers throughout Britain. Your local education authority will also have a list of teachers in your area.

BRITISH KEEP-FIT CONFEDERATION, 27 Norton Drive, Parklands, Stirchley, Telford, Shropshire TF3 1EJ. Tel: 0952 594503.
This organization is dedicated to competitive keep-fit, believing that challenge stimulates the will to do better. Any keep-fit group or enthusiast aged from 15 to 55 can contact the Confederation at the above address.

ALCOHOLICS ANONYMOUS, 11 Redcliffe Gardens, London SW10. Tel: 01-834 8202 for the London area; 01-352 9779 for the rest of Britain.
The AA celebrates its 50th anniversary in 1985. Anyone who needs help with a drinking problem should ring one of

the above numbers, and the Association will arrange for someone in your area to contact you. Having met you, your contact will take you to a meeting and follow it up; after that it will be up to you.

STANDING CONFERENCE ON DRUG ABUSE, 1/4 Hatton Place, Hatton Garden, London EC1N 8ND. Tel: 01-430 2341.
This registered charity co-ordinates the activities of non-statutory agencies working in the drugs field and offers advice on setting up services, funding and training. It will provide information and advice on services throughout Britain for anyone who has a drug problem, and a list of useful publications on request.

Chapter 6 SEX AND SEXUALITY

BRITISH ASSOCIATION OF PSYCHOTHERAPISTS, 121 Hendon Lane, London N3 3PR. Tel: 01-346 1747.
Contact the Association for a list of sex therapists in your area who, as long as you also have a medical practitioner looking after you, should be able to advise you.

NATIONAL MARRIAGE GUIDANCE COUNCILS and BROOK ADVISORY CENTRES can also help (see pages 139 and 144).

Chapter 7 WORK

VOLUNTARY WORK INFORMATION SERVICES, 68 Chalton Street, London NW1. Tel: 01-388 0241.
This organization will supply information and a list of volunteer bureaux in London.

VOLUNTEER CENTRE, 29 Lower Kings Road, Berkhamsted, Herts HP4 2AB. Tel: 04427 73311.
The Centre has a directory of voluntary units throughout Britain and will advise anyone interested in doing voluntary work.

OPEN UNIVERSITY, PO Box 48, Milton Keynes MK7 6AB. Tel: 0908 74066.

You need no qualifications to register with the Open University, and you study at home. Courses range from short ones of eight weeks (on subjects such as parenting and energy-saving) to three-, four- and five-year degree programmes. You are taught by correspondence, with the additional help of radio and television programmes. Fees vary from £20 for a short course to £200 per annum for a full degree course.

TOPS (Training Opportunities Scheme)
The scheme consists of courses for re-training or updating skills and is available to anyone over 19 who has been away from full-time education for at least two years and has not done a TOPS course within the past three years. The training is free and a tax-free allowance is paid to those attending a course. The many courses last for differing lengths of time. Further details may be requested from the Manpower Services Commission, Selkirk House, 166 High Holborn, London WC1 6PF, tel: 01-836 1213; or any Jobcentre in your area.

Evening classes
Floodlight, a magazine listing evening classes in the London area, is available from newsagents or from the ILEA, Room 77, County Hall, London SE1 7PB, tel: 01-633 1066, and costs £1.00.
    Outside London you can obtain information about evening classes from the local education authority.

Chapter 8 CHILDREN

The following organizations, listed on pages 138–44, can help with conciliation and counselling:
NATIONAL FAMILY CONCILIATION COUNCIL
DIVORCE, CONCILIATION AND ADVISORY SERVICE
WESTMINSTER PASTORAL ASSOCIATION
FAMILY WELFARE ASSOCIATION
NATIONAL COUNCIL FOR ONE-PARENT FAMILIES.

The following can advise on supplementary benefit and other money matters:
NATIONAL ASSOCIATION OF WIDOWS (page 138)

NATIONAL COUNCIL FOR ONE-PARENT FAMILIES
(page 144)
CHILD POVERTY ACTION GROUP (page 142)
CITIZENS' ADVICE BUREAUX (page 146)

The following can advise and help with babysitting:

MOTHERS' UNION, SOCIAL CONCERN (page 138)
SINGLEHANDED LTD (page 146)
GINGERBREAD (page 145)

For help or practical advice on home matters, contact:

MOTHERS' UNION (SOCIAL CONCERN) (page 138)
FAMILY WELFARE ASSOCIATION (page 143)
SALVATION ARMY (page 143)

The following organizations will arrange holidays for parents and children, or children on their own:

MOTHERS' UNION (SOCIAL CONCERN) (page 138)
NATIONAL COUNCIL FOR THE DIVORCED AND
   SEPARATED (page 141)
SINGLHANDED LTD (page 146)
GINGERBREAD (page 145)
ENGLISH TOURIST BOARD (page 154)

PRE-SCHOOL PLAYGROUPS ASSOCIATION, Alford
House, Aveline Street, London SE11 5DH, tel: 01-582 8871;
and 16 Sandyford Place, Glasgow G3, tel: 041 221 4148.
There are 360 branches all over Britain, which will advise on
starting and running a playgroup and supply leaflets and
books on the subject.

NATIONAL OUT-OF-SCHOOL ALLIANCE, Oxford
House, Derbyshire Street, London E2 6HG. Tel: 01-739
4787.
This organization can supply details of after-school and
holiday playgroups and centres, and can suggest ideas for
amusing children during school holidays.

ADVISORY CENTRE FOR EDUCATION, 18 Victoria Park
Square, London E2 9PB. Tel: 01-980 4596.
This centre offers advice on educational procedures (where
to go to find out about local schools, for example) by letter

or phone. It produces a monthly magazine, information sheets and handbooks and can advise on the law as applied to education (suspension, for instance) or special schools.

NATIONAL STEPFAMILY ASSOCIATION, Maris House, Trumpington, Cambridge CB2 2LB. Tel: 0223 841306.
The Association offers practical help, support, information and advice to any member who is, or is likely to become, part of a stepfamily.

Chapter 9 SOCIAL LIFE

NATIONAL FEDERATION OF SOLO CLUBS, Room 8, Ruskin Chambers, 191 Corporation Street, Birmingham B4 6RY. Tel: 021 236 2879 (also 0384 67137, evenings).
The Federation has clubs all over Britain, charging an average £1.00 annual membership. It organizes outings, social evenings, events which children may attend, and so on. All single people are welcome.

ASSOCIATION OF BRITISH INTRODUCTION AGENCIES, 29 Manchester Street, London W1.
The Association's members, which include marriage bureaux and friendship and computer agencies, are all bona fide and therefore preferable to those not included on its membership list.

DATELINE, 23 Abingdon Road, London W8 Tel: 01-938 1011.
Dateline has 35,000 members all over Britain and is the main computer agency in the UK. Although the whole process of matching people is done on computer, it is not completely impersonal because you can chat to someone there before and after you join, and if you have any worries.

Be honest when you fill in your questionnaire, otherwise you will be wasting your money. On payment of £65 (one year's membership) your details are run through the computer to find a match of the opposite sex. A list of the six most compatible people is sent to you and it is up to you to contact them.

If you are extremely specific about the person you wish to meet, a match will be more difficult to find. If less than three matches result from your first run, you will be given another one free of charge. Otherwise, after the first run, further names cost £2.00. Some people who want a busy social life ask for new runs every month.

Often it is hard to find suitable people for women over 50, because there are so many more of them than men. In such cases, Dateline does not accept money until the first run has been made.

The fees are reduced for women under 25 (because the proportion of men to women is about 2-1) to £45, and for men over 50, because at that age men are in the minority. If no matches come up on the computer, Dateline will refund the fee.

NEXUS, Nexus House, Blackstock Road, London N4. Tel: 01-359 7656.

Nexus, established for ten years, has 10,000 members and branches not only throughout Great Britain but also in America, Australia and Germany. There are main offices in Glasgow, Manchester, Leeds, Bristol, Hove and Oxford. It is an association of unattached people, open to all those who are on their own – widowed, divorced or separated. Events are organized throughout Britain, and the monthly diary includes coffee mornings, social gatherings, outings and visits to the theatre.

On joining Nexus you will be sent details of their social calendar, the address of every venue, and the names and telephone numbers of 'Link' members who will make it their business to get you into the swing of things. They will meet you first and take you to a party, if you do not want to go somewhere unknown on your own, introduce you to other members and generally look after you. If you enjoy the set-up, you could well become a 'Link' member yourself.

Nexus has regular meetings and 'open invitation' events which are listed in a monthly bulletin as well as impromptu events which you will find out about through the people you meet. You can meet members visiting from abroad and, if you travel abroad yourself, be put in touch with members in that country. There is also a list of members willing to advise on anything from car mechanics to hanging curtains to finance. If you have a particular knowledge of any subject, you can put your name on the list so that other people can contact you for advice.

Nexus will help members to organize events and out-ings, or find people with similar interests if you want to start something new.

Membership is £61.20 for the first year and thereafter £36. Six months' membership costs £42.60.

NETWORK CAMPUS CLUB, 32 Great Marlborough Street, London W1 Tel: 01-437 1454.

This club is run by an American, Judith Rose, and was started in early 1984. At present it is based in London, but expansion into other parts of Britain is likely. There are two parts of Network. The Campus runs seminars on a variety of subjects from 'life-planning' to self-hypnosis, public speaking, understanding computers and losing weight. These take place regularly in the evening. The Network Club is the social side. It organizes regular events such as trips to the theatre, dinners at restaurants known for national cuisines, backgammon evenings and ice-skating; and theme weekends (centred on, for example, photogra-phy, tennis or human relationships).

The club is not only for singles, but also for couples who are looking for new interests, a chance to meet new people and find out about new places.

Annual membership is £25, which includes regular newsletters and two free seminars. The seminars are not restricted to members, though they cost less if you are one, so you could go along to one that interests you, find out more about what goes on and what the people are like before you join.

Other organizations which can provide a social life for single people are:

NATIONAL ASSOCIATION OF WIDOWS (page 138)
NATIONAL COUNCIL FOR THE DIVORCED AND
  SEPARATED (page 141)
ASSOCIATION OF SEPARATED AND DIVORCED
  CATHOLICS (page 141)
SINGLEHANDED LTD (page 146)
GINGERBREAD (page 145)
CITIZENS' ADVICE BUREAUX (page 146) will also be able
to advise you of bona fide singles clubs in your area.

There are two singles magazines currently on the market: *Singles*, based at 23 Abingdon Road, London W8, tel: 01-938 1011, which has been established since 1976; and *Personal*, of 12–18 Paul Street, London EC2A 4JS, tel: 01-247 8233, which was launched in October 1984. Both contain articles relevant to single people, personal classified advertisements, which are carefully vetted, holiday advertisements and so on. All replies to small ads are to box numbers, so you need not reveal to the world at large that you are looking for friends.

Holidays

PASSPORT OFFICE, Clive House, 70–78 Petty France, London SW1. Tel: 01-213 3434.
The Passport Office will answer any queries you have about passports. Passport application forms can be obtained from all main post offices and from travel agents.

BACCANALIA, 75 Albert Road, Richmond, Surrey TW10 6DJ. Tel: 01-940 0109.
Baccanalia runs holidays at various price levels for 23–70-year-olds who are on their own. It tries to organize well-balanced groups going, for example, to Benidorm or Barbados. It also organizes nights out in London; weekend breaks – like informal houseparties – in England; and Christmas and New Year events.

SOLOS, 41 Watford Way, Hendon, London NW4 3JH. Tel: 01-202 0855.
This company offers holidays for 'independent over-30s' and organizes special-interest weekends focusing on, for example, bridge, sightseeing or music, and trips at times such as Christmas.

CLUB 18–30, 24 Oval Road, London NW1. Tel: 01-267 0941
This company runs holidays in several countries for young singles, featuring excursions, entertainment and social and other activities.

HOLIDAY CARE SERVICE, 2 Old Bank Chambers, Station Road, Horley, Surrey. Tel: 0293 774535.

Holiday Care Service provides information on holidays for single parents and their children, and can also offer advice on financial problems.

The following companies run special-interest holidays, not necessarily for singles:
Best Western (Getaway brochure); tel: 01-940 9766 or 041-204 1794.
British Rail ('Great Little Escapes'); tel: 0904 28992.
Embassy (Leisure Learning); tel: 0283 66587.
Ladbroke (Lazydays); tel: 0923 46465.
Further information is available from travel agents.

VACATION WORK INTERNATIONAL, 9 Park End Street, Oxford OX1 1HJ.
This company arranges for parties of people to work abroad: looking after children, picking grapes or working on a farm, for example. You have to work hard, but just being abroad and meeting new people could be enough of a break to make it a holiday.

The following associations also organize holidays:

MOTHERS' UNION, SOCIAL CONCERN (page 138)
NATIONAL COUNCIL FOR THE DIVORCED AND
   SEPARATED (page 141)
BROKEN RITES (page 142)
SINGLEHANDED LTD (page 146)
GINGERBREAD (page 145)

Chapter 10 HOMOSEXUAL RELATIONSHIPS

CAMPAIGN FOR HOMOSEXUAL EQUALITY, 274 Upper Street, London N1 Tel: 01-359 3973.
This association aims to stop discrimination against men and women based on sexual preference. Though CHE cannot itself provide advice to individuals, there are over 100 affiliated groups in England and Wales which help and provide meeting places for gays. The above office can put you in touch with one of these groups.

SCOTTISH HOMOSEXUAL RIGHTS GROUP, 60 Broughton Street, Edinburgh EH1 3SA.
This is a similar organization to CHE, offering help and advice to anyone with a homosexual problem. It has two information centres and several branches which hold weekly discussions and socials. The advisory service numbers (evenings only) are:
Edinburgh: tel: 031 556 4049
Glasgow: tel: 041 221 8372
Aberdeen: tel: 0224 586869 (Wednesdays only)
Dundee: tel: 0382 24591 (Tuesdays only).

GAY BEREAVEMENT PROJECT, Unitarian Rooms, Hoop Lane, London NW11 8BS.
Formed in 1981, the aims of the Project are to help gay people who have lost their partners through death. It offers practical help and emotional support, immediately after the death if required.
    Its advisers are carefully selected for their understanding and experience. They will talk to you on the phone and listen to your problems, help with registering the death and coping with funeral arrangements, and make every effort to help you through this unhappy time. They can find sympathetic clergy and funeral directors, and be with you to give support at the funeral when you might be feeling isolated from other friends and relations. Their numbers are available from the Gay Switchboard.

GAY SWITCHBOARD. Tel: 01-837 7324.
The Gay Switchboard can provide your first contact with more specialized organizations. It provides a 24-hour service, and holds details of flat-shares and entertainments as well as giving advice. There are 40 independent switchboards throughout the world, details of which can be obtained from the London number or through Directory Enquiries. You can chat to anyone on the switchboard if you want to talk or seek advice.

1066 GAY COMMUNITY ORGANIZATION, c/o Norman Cross, Hastings Voluntary Services, 48 Cambridge Gardens, Hastings, Sussex.
This is a small organization which hopes to inspire the formation of others in different areas. It supports married

and divorced gays, both those who knew they were gay during their marriage and those who have only discovered subsequently. The organization will talk to people and help them, especially if they feel isolated, and put them in touch with appropriate advice sources.

There are monthly meetings at which gays can chat to those who have had similar experiences. Quite often people have found some relief in coming to these meetings when they have been frightened of going elsewhere.

LONDON FRIENDS. Tel: 01-359 7371.
Despite its name, this is a national organization, with nearly 30 branches, which offers a befriending and counselling service in the evenings from 7.30 pm to 10.00 pm. You can drop into the coffee bar for a chat with one of their 80 volunteers, or with other people in the same position as you. The Friends will also put you in touch with local gay groups.

Chapter 11 PRACTICALITIES

DAILY TELEGRAPH INFORMATION SERVICE (tel: 01-353 4242) provides information by telephone. If you are looking for the address or telephone number of a particular organization, or want to find out whether there is an association concerned with a particular cause or subject, the staff will do their best to help you.

LAW SOCIETY, 113 Chancery Lane, London WC2A 1PL. Tel: 01-242 1222.
This is the professional association of solicitors. It will deal with complaints against any of its members and advise on legal aid for civil matters. It publishes leaflets on buying and selling homes, on seeing a solicitor, and on legal aid.

LAW SOCIETY OF SCOTLAND, Law Society's Hall, 26 Drumsheugh Gardens, Edinburgh EH3 7YR, is the professional association of solicitors in Scotland.

LEGAL AID DEPARTMENT, The Law Society, 29 Red Lion Street, London WC1. Tel: 01-405 6991.
Staff will refer you to solicitors working under the legal aid

scheme, and help and advise you if you want to know more about legal aid.

SOLICITORS' FAMILY LAW ASSOCIATION, 154 Fleet Street, London EC4 7ZX. Tel: 01-353 3290.
This is a professional association of solicitors who specialize in matrimonial and family law. It was formed because some solicitors felt that many were taking a too litigious view of divorce at the expense of the individual involved. They have formed a Code of Practice and their 400 members, spread all over Britain, are able to use each other's knowledge to increase their own expertise.

If you think you need better, or more, advice than you are receiving, or would like to know which solicitor in your area is a member of this association, write to the Secretary, Mr P. Grose-Hodge, at the above address.

LAW CENTRES. These offer free advice and information. They are in many areas, and the address of your local one can be found in the telephone directory or obtained from the Citizens' Advice Bureau.

DEPARTMENT OF ENERGY, Thames House South, Millbank, London SW1. Tel: 01-211 6361.
Write or ring for their leaflets on saving fuel.

BUILDING SOCIETIES' ASSOCIATION, 3 Savile Row, London W1. Tel: 01-437 0655.
This association publishes a leaflet, *Hints For Home Buyers*, and other more detailed booklets about borrowing money and how to buy a house. All are available free of charge.

NEW HOMES MARKETING BOARD, 82 New Cavendish Street, London W1M 8AD. Tel: 01-580 5588.
If you are moving to a different area and are interested in buying a new home, this board has compiled a guide, covering over 3000 developments, including properties for single people, listed alphabetically by county and town. It includes brief details of each property, and an indication of price, and you can request full information on up to nine specific developments.

BRITISH ASSOCIATION OF REMOVERS, 277 Gray's Inn Road, London WC1X 8SY.
The Association has produced a colour leaflet advising on problems that may arise when moving home, and a list of members in each area. Send a large stamped addressed envelope for a copy.

NATIONAL FEDERATION OF HOUSING ASSOCIATIONS, 175 Gray's Inn Road, London WC1X 8UP. Tel: 01-278 6571.
The Federation gives advice and information on housing associations all over Britain.

LOCAL OMBUDSMEN will investigate complaints against local authorities. You may apply personally only if a councillor will not refer your complaint.

Further information can be obtained from the Commission for Local Administration, 21 Queen Anne's Gate, London SW1H 9BU, tel: 01-222 5622; 29 Castlegate, York YO1 1RN, tel: 0904 30151; Derwen House, Court Road, Bridgend, Mid-Glam CF31 1BN, tel: 0656 61325; Princes House, 5 Shandwick Place, Edinburgh EH2 4RG, tel: 031 229 4472.

OFFICE OF FAIR TRADING, Room 310C, Field House, Bream's Buildings, London EC4A 1PR.
This organization has a leaflet entitled *Home Improvements* which gives guidelines on how to protect yourself against 'cowboys', contracts, cancellation rights and legal obligations (free from the above address). It also produces leaflets on how to cope with doorstep salesmen; what to do if you buy something faulty; and how to take a complaint further if you get no satisfaction from the retailer or manufacturer.

TRADE ASSOCIATIONS. Trade associations will provide lists of members in each area. You can also refer to them if you have any complaints against their members.

ROYAL INSTITUTE OF BRITISH ARCHITECTS, 66 Portland Place, London W1N 4AD. Tel: 01-637 8991.

FEDERATION OF MASTER BUILDERS, 19 Station Road, South Norwood, London SE25. Tel: 01-771 5451.

There are also several offices in other parts of Britain; the London office will advise you of your nearest one.

ELECTRICAL CONTRACTORS' ASSOCIATION, 34 Palace Court, London W2 4HY, tel: 01-229 1266; and 23 Heriot Row, Edinburgh EH3 6EW, tel: 031 225 7221.

NATIONAL ASSOCIATION OF PLUMBING, HEATING AND MECHANICAL CONTRACTORS, 6 Gate Street, London WC2A 3HX, tel: 01-405 2678; and 2 Walker Street, Edinburgh EH3 7LP, tel: 031 225 2255.

ROYAL INSTITUTION OF CHARTERED SURVEYORS, 12 Great George Street, London SW1P 3AD. Tel: 01-222 7000.

Chapter 12 MONEY

INSTITUTE OF CHARTERED ACCOUNTANTS (England and Wales), PO Box 433, Chartered Accountants' Hall, Moorgate Place, London EC2P 2BJ. Tel: 01-628 7060.

INSTITUTE OF CHARTERED ACCOUNTANTS (Scotland), 27 Queen Street, Edinburgh EH2 1LA.
These will supply details of member accountants and help with complaints.

If you have a complaint against your insurance company, and it is a member of one of the following organizations, you can contact the relevant one for help:

INSURANCE OMBUDSMAN BUREAU, 31 Southampton Row, London WC1B 5JH. Tel: 01-242 8613.

BRITISH INSURANCE ASSOCIATION, Aldermarry House, Queen Street, London EC4N 1TU. Tel: 01-248 4477.

BRITISH INSURANCE BROKERS' ASSOCIATION, 14 Bevis Marks, London EC3. Tel: 01-623 9043.
You can get a list of insurance brokers in your area from this association, which can also provide advice.

BANKING INFORMATION SERVICE, 10 Lombard Street, London EC3V 9AP. Tel: 01-626 8486.
Staff will advise on all banking matters; the information

service operates on behalf of the six major British clearing banks.

PROBATE PERSONAL APPLICATION DEPARTMENT, Golden Cross House, Duncannon Street, London WC2N 4JF, tel: 01-214 3015, for England, Wales and Northern Ireland. For Scotland, contact the Sheriff's Court.
If you want to apply for probate yourself, the above office can supply a list of probate offices which have a personal application department with special staff, forms and procedures to help. Or you can obtain Form PR48, which gives you a list of offices and guidelines on procedure, free of charge, from Somerset House, The Strand, London WC2; or from Oyez stationery branches, where you will have to pay for it.

MONEY MATTERS, Ringwood House, Ireton Avenue, Walton-on-Thames, Surrey KT12 1EN. Tel: 0932 221286.
This is run by a group of women for women to inform them about money, insurance and the financial side of divorce. Courses are held throughout the year.

CHAPTER 14

Reference

This chapter details specific payments, charges and benefits which are of particular relevance to those who have
been bereaved, are divorced or separated, or head a one-
parent family. All this information, though correct at the
time or writing, is highly vulnerable to alteration by government legislation in the light of inflation, etc.

SOCIAL SECURITY BENEFITS
Most payments are increased annually.

Child benefit	Each child, £6.85 per week (leaflet CH.1).
One-parent benefit	First child only, £4.25 per week (leaflet CH. 11).
Child's special allowance	Each child, £7.65 per week (leaflet N1.93).
Family income supplement	Payable if weekly income is below £90 for one-child family; £100 for two children; £110 for three. Maximum payment for family with one child £23 per week; £2 for each subsequent child. (Leaflet FIS.1.)
Supplementary benefit	Claim if weekly income of single householder under 60 after paying rent is £28.05; add £9.60 for children under 11; £14.35 for 11–15-year-olds; £17.30 for 16–17-year-olds; £22.45 for those aged 18 or over. For single householder over 60, £35.70 per week, which is the same as the long-term rate.

Long-term rates: single person, £35.70 per week; for children aged 16–17, £21.90; over 18, £28.55.

To qualify you must not have savings over £3000 in any category (leaflet SB.1.)

Unemployment benefit	£28.45 per week (leaflet NI.12).
Sickness benefit	£27.25 per week (leaflet NI.16).
Widow's benefits	Widow's allowance, £50.10 per week. Widowed mother's allowance, £35.80 per week. Widow's pension, £35.80 per week. Age-related widow's pension: between ages 40–49 the pension increases yearly from £10.74 to £33.29 per week (leaflets NP.35 and NP.36). Widow's child benefit, £7.65 per week.
Death grant	£30 (leaflet NI.49).

Free leaflets on social security benefits are available from post offices and social security offices; or write to DHSS Leaflets, PO Box 21, Stanmore, Middlesex HA7 1AY.

For problems with child and one-parent benefits, write to Child Benefit Centre (Washington), PO Box 1, Newcastle-Upon-Tyne NE88 1AA.

For queries on Family Income Supplement, write to FIS, Freepost, Blackpool FY2 0BR.

HOW EARNINGS AFFECT PENSIONS

The earnings limit, before it affects your state pension, is £70.00 a week. Between £70 and £108 the pension is progressively reduced, and at the higher figure you lose it altogether. Earnings means gross weekly salary before tax, less certain allowable expenses (such as the cost of having a dependent relative at home).

163

HOW EARNINGS AFFECT SUPPLEMENTARY BENEFIT

The first £4 of your net weekly earnings is ignored. ('Net' means after taking off tax, national insurance contributions, cost of travel to work, union dues, cost of looking after your child, 15p for each meal at work and other 'reasonable' work expenses.) If your net earnings are between £4 and £20, 50p is taken off your weekly benefit for every £1 you earn; after £20 you have the same amount taken off as you earn.

TAX ALLOWANCES (to year 5 April 1985)

Single person's allowance £2,005 per annum, or if over 65, with income below a certain level, £2,490 per annum. This 'age allowance' is reduced by £2 for every £3 of income when the total income exceeds £8,100 per annum.

Single parent's additional allowance, £1,150 per annum.

Widow's bereavement allowance, £1,150 per annum.

MAINTENANCE

Small maintenance payments are payments below £33 a week or £143 a month in favour of one party or a child of the marriage; or £18 a week or £78 a month if paid to the mother for a child's benefit. These are all paid without tax being deducted at source.

DEATH CERTIFICATE CHARGES

The first two are free. After that extra standard death certificates cost £1.80 each; special death certificates £1.50 each.

BURIAL AND CREMATION CHARGES

A burial with a service beforehand costs £33; without a service it is £22. Payments to the gravedigger, the organist and choir are extra. Charges for having the body buried in a parish other than the deceased's own will usually be higher.

The fee payable to a Church of England clergyman for performing a service in the cemetery is £16.50. Fees to other denominational clergy vary. The cost of cemetery burials also varies: charges will be displayed at the cemetery; your undertakers will also have details of them.

Each crematorium has its own scale of fees ranging from

£20 to £130. These usually include the fee for the signing of Form F and the use of the chapel.

PROBATE

The court fee and departmental fee, which is paid if the grant is taken out without a solicitor, are both calculated on the amount of the net estate. There is no court fee on an estate of less than £10,000; from £10,000 to £25,000, the fee is £40; from £25,000 to £40,000, it is £80; then £2.50 per £1000 up to £100,000. For an estate of more than £100,000 the court fee is £250 plus £50 for every additional £100,000.

The departmental fee starts at £1 for an estate of £500 rising to £10 for £10,000; over that add £1 for every additional £1,000.

Probate is not always necessary for an estate of less than £5,000. Capital Transfer Tax is paid on any estate of over £64,000.

Bibliography

BEREAVEMENT
Living With Grief, Dr Tony Lake, Sheldon Press.
Widow, Lynn Caine, MacDonald & Jane's. (A personal account of widowhood.)
All in the End is Harvest (an anthology for those who grieve), edited by Agnes Whitaker, Darton, Longman and Todd.
What to Do When Someone Dies, Consumers' Association.

DIVORCE AND SEPARATION
Divorce and Separation, Angela Willans, Sheldon Press.
Divorce, Legal Procedures and Financial Facts, Consumers' Association.
Breaking Even: Divorce, Your Children and You, Jacqueline Burgoyne, Penguin.
Divorce and Your Children, Anne Hooper, Unwin Paperbacks.

WORK
Working Abroad, Daily Telegraph.
Residential Short Courses, National Institute of Adult Continuing Education, 19B De Montfort Street, Leicester LE1 7GE.
Earning Money at Home, Consumers' Association.
(See also below under holidays.)

WHERE TO GO FOR HELP
The Sunday Times Self-Help Directory, edited by Oliver Gillie, Angela Price and Sharon Robinson, Granada. (A list of groups and organizations throughout Britain.)

HOME
Rights Guide for Homeowners, Jo Tunnard and Clare Whately, published by the Child Poverty Action Group (see page 142).

Which? Way to Cut Heating Bills, Consumers' Association.
Which? Way to Buy, Sell and Move House, Consumers' Association. (Covers everything from accidents to insulation and gardening.)
How to Cope in Your Home, Barbara Chandler, Ward Lock. (A clear and simple guide to mending fuses, changing light bulbs, general maintenance, etc.)
The Householder's Action Guide, Consumers' Association. (A guide to any problem that may occur if you own or rent a home.)

COOKING
Man in the Kitchen, Alan Curthoys and Judy Ridgway, Judy Piatkus.
Good Housekeeping Cooking for Today, Octopus. (Techniques, equipment, recipes, entertaining, wines, serving, catering, parties, storage etc.)
Cookery in Colour, Marguerite Patten, Hamlyn. (A simple cookbook for beginners.)
Easy Cooking for One or Two, Louise Davies, Penguin.
Short-cut Cookbook, Katie Stewart, Pan.
The Cook Book, Terence and Caroline Conran, Mitchell Beazley. (A definitive book on the purchase and preparation of food.)
Eat Your Way to Health, Vicki Peterson, Penguin.

HOLIDAYS
Summer Jobs Abroad and Summer Jobs in Britain, Vacation Work Publishers, Oxford.
Leisure Interests/Activity Holidays, Activity Holiday Associates, Somerset.
Activity and Hobby Holidays, English Tourist Board.

MONEY
Making the Most of Your Money, Louise Botting and Vincent Duggleby, Orbis.
Money Matters for Women, Liz McDonnell, Collins/Willow.
Moneywoman, Georgina O'Hara, Sphere.
Your Social Security, Frances Bennett, Penguin.
Daily Telegraph Guide to Income Tax, Collins.

PROBATE
Wills and Probate, Consumers' Association.